Why violence?

Why violence?

A philosophical interpretation
by Sergio Cotta

Translated by Giovanni Gullace

UNIVERSITY PRESSES OF FLORIDA
University of Florida Press
Gainesville

English translation copyright 1985 by University Presses of Florida.
All rights reserved.
Published by permission of L. U. Japadre editore.
Originally published as
Perchè la violenza? Una interpretazione filosofica.
Copyright 1978 by L. U. Japadre editore — L'Aquila

Library of Congress Cataloging in Publication Data

Cotta, Sergio.E
 Why violence?

 Translation of: Perché la violenza.
 Includes index.
 I. Violence. I. Title.
HM281.C6713   1985   303.6'2   84-25779
ISBN 0-8130-0804-2

UNIVERSITY PRESSES OF FLORIDA is the central agency for scholarly publishing of the State of Florida's university system, producing books selected for publication by the faculty editorial committees of Florida's nine public universities: Florida A&M University (Tallahassee), Florida Atlantic University (Boca Raton), Florida International University (Miami), Florida State University (Tallahassee), University of Central Florida (Orlando), University of Florida (Gainesville), University of North Florida (Jacksonville), University of South Florida (Tampa), University of West Florida (Pensacola).
 Orders for books published by all member presses of University Presses of Florida should be addressed to University Presses of Florida, 15 NW 15th Street, Gainesville, Florida 32603.

Contents

Foreword

by Dante Germino

Sergio Cotta, professor and director of the Institute for the Study of the Philosophy of Law at the University of Rome, has written a compelling account of the widespread phenomenon of violence in the contemporary world. He has produced a work that is at once analytical and ontological, detached and committed, rooted in the history of political and legal philosophy, and relevant to understanding this morning's newspaper, a work that draws impressively on a variety of sources, including Machiavelli, Vico, Kant, Hegel, Marx, Heidegger, and Sartre as well as from Benjamin, Simmel, and the Italian philosopher Capograssi—in sum, a work that defies stereotyped classifications and ideological positions.

The first part of Professor Cotta's book might be described as a phenomenology of violence. He takes issue with both those writers who define violence too broadly and those who define it too narrowly. The difficulty with the first group is that if all politics and history are seen in terms of violence, then the very distinction between violent and nonviolent action becomes meaningless. What Cotta calls the "apocalyptic" theory of violence holds that all institutions of modern "repressive" society are manifestations of violence, for they "violate" the humanity of man by manipulating, indoctrinating, and regimenting him, even if the means used are "peaceful." For Cotta, this radical position is absurd, for it abolishes the very distinction between public force and private violence as well as the distinction between violence and nonviolence.

While the formulators of contemporary radical revolutionary thought are mostly nonviolent people themselves, there is a direct connection between their doctrines and the actions of groups like the Red Brigades and the Baader-Meinhof gang, he argues. Indeed, Cotta thinks that the current widespread exaltation of violence and its equation with morality is unprecedented in the history of thought. Hitherto, even revolutionaries such as Marx, Lenin, and Mao endorsed violence only as a grim necessity to achieve the victory of the revolution. They viewed violence coldly and calculatingly as a *means* to achieve an *end*. The new "revolutionaries," on the other hand, glorify violence itself as their end. The violent revolution is to be permanent.

While exposing this variant of radical revolutionary thought to the cold light of reality, Cotta is careful not to define violence too narrowly as exclusively the work of "private," "unauthorized" groups. He points out that the distinction between "legitimate force" (by constituted public authority) and illegitimate violence (issuing from private groups) obscures the truth that even constitutionally established public authorities can fall into patterns of activity that violate the dignity of individuals. Ritualistic cries for "law and order" may themselves contribute to a climate of violence.

In his masterful and moving conclusion, Professor Cotta considers the question posed in the book's title: why is there violence? Ranging over such topics as the influence of Rousseau's voluntarism on democratic doctrine, the advent of industrial, technological society, the "activist historicism" of Marx, the overthrow of what he calls the "juridical measure" by a legal philosophy that reduces law to the expression of a particular will, and "absolute subjectivism" in twentieth-century philosophy, Cotta's analysis of this question is brilliant and complex. He concludes that violence is "an unregulated, nondialogic, and noncoexistential counter-activity," a phenomenon that can be described only in terms of negations and one that each individual who "has respect for man and thus for himself" has a personal responsibility to try to overcome. Cotta bids us to heed the "radical request of the ethics of brotherhood," to recognize the dignity of the Other, and to reverse the "reversal of values" manifesting itself in one strand of the modern intellectual tradition.

Professor Cotta's philosophical framework and flair for nuance bring a new dimension and a refreshing lucidity to the discussion of this important issue. His magisterial study of violence is one of the major works on political theory published in the last decade. As the first of Sergio Cotta's books to be translated into English, *Why Violence? A Philosophical Interpretation* is significant in another way: it introduces the English-speaking public to one of Europe's foremost political and legal philosophers.

Sergio Cotta was born in Florence in 1920 of a Piedmontese family. During the resistance movement against the Fascist dictatorship, he organized and commanded a Partisan brigade in the Piedmont region. Before being called to the University of Rome, he taught at the Universities of Perugia, Trieste, and Florence. Professor Cotta is president of the Italian Society for Legal and Political Philosophy, and in 1982 he was appointed a fellow of the Woodrow Wilson Center. He has published a dozen books in Italian and French, among them *La sfida tecnologica* (1968) and *L'uomo tolemaico* (1975), both of which concern the problems of technological civilization. His most recent book, *Il Diritto nell' esistenza* [Law and Existence], is in press as this foreword is being written.

Preface

To speak of violence nowadays is not a novelty; the theme is almost obligatory for anyone concerned with everyday events. This small book, however, was not conceived on the spur of the moment. It has a more remote origin: not only because it developed slowly, over many years, through seminars and lectures (at the Universities of Pamplona and Paris, at cultural circles in Rome and Florence), and above all in two courses at the School of Advanced Studies in the Philosophy of Law of the University of Rome, but also because, like others of my generation, I have gone through, and am still going through, the experience of violence so rampant in our century. Violence has constantly been intertwined with my personal life, at times through the testimony of others, at times through direct observation, at times through personal involvement. To write about it, therefore, means to bring together the threads of memories and reflections, both close and remote, of an entire lifetime. It is not in the power of one individual to escape the violence of an epoch, much less to put an end to it. But to try to overcome it is, I believe, a fundamental personal commitment for anyone endowed with a sense of respect for man and, consequently, for himself. Undoubtedly, reflection is not enough to eradicate violence from one's own soul. One must subject it to analysis, disassemble its mechanisms, evaluate its justifications and promises. One would otherwise run the risk of falling into error, as often happens, by mistaking violence for something other than what it is and even yielding to its fascination.

I have not proposed to myself to examine the entire range of violence or to illustrate all the situations from which it can spring; it would have been a boundless undertaking to which many others have already devoted themselves. I was deeply concerned with two clearly limited objectives. The first was to throw light on the structure of violent behavior by beginning, as I customarily do, with a survey of its phenomenology. The second was to go beyond the *how* of violence and seek to understand and discuss the *why* of that which is, in my opinion, the genuinely new aspect of today's situation: the favorable appraisal of violence. These are limited objectives, I repeat, but in no way peripheral if one wishes to achieve the critical detachment so necessary in the face of such an intriguing phenomenon and the fatalistic atmosphere in which it immerses us all.

For his sensitive translation of this book, I wish to acknowledge my gratitude to Professor Giovanni Gullace of the State University of New York, whose distinguished career as a scholar and translator has earned him both the Order of Merit from the Italian government and the title of Chevalier de l'Ordre des Palmes Académiques from the French government. I am honored to have *Why Violence? A Philosophical Interpretation* added to Professor Gullace's impressive list of translations, which includes Benedetto Croce's *Poetry and Literature* and Giovanni Gentile's *The Philosophy of Art*.

Finally, I would like to thank my friend and colleague Professor Dante Germino of the University of Virigina for his generosity in bringing my work to the attention of the English-speaking public. My old friendship with him has grown stronger in the stimulating meetings of the Institut International de Philosophie Politique.

Rome, January 1985   S. C.

Chapter 1
Today's violence: new or old?

Current viewpoints

The subject of violence has already made its way into the daily conversation of our times; it leads to reflections and inquiries, is at the center of politicians' preoccupations and the worries of private citizens, gives inspiration for novels and films. That is not surprising, for violence is so widespread and frightening in all aspects and at all levels of today's life that press, radio, and television never stop reminding us of it.[1] Violence rages at the level of international relations in the form of war, or more often, in the form of merciless guerrilla warfare; at the level of internal relations it takes the form of political terrorism, ideological persecution, and private banditry. Violence hides in the antinomies of our very ways of life, which are lawless and mass-dominated, intellectualized and emotive, artificial and natural, torn apart between the pressing urge (often brought about artificially) for productive activism

1. See the well-informed "Chronique de la violence," periodically published in *Études polémologiques*, directed by G. Bouthoul.

and a spreading desire for amusement and happiness. I am referring above all to industrialized countries. Violence enters even into our habits of speaking and communicating: in the amplified and dehumanized screaming from loudspeakers at political rallies and in places of amusement, or simply in the unbearable noises of the streets, in the constant use of deliberately desecrating and cruel words and images that are brutally applied to anyone, without restraint, respect, or decency. How often people, by substituting the language of war for the language of dialogue, inject the words "struggle," "battle," "victory," into every insignificant discussion or controversy even when it occurs among inactive individuals or groups!

In this situation, public moral sense and private moral sense seem to be overwhelmed by the spreading of violence, which they oppose with ineffective talk or useless sermonizing, when in fact they themselves are conquered by it and act as its agents. Since violence appears to dominate life in our times, a judgment on it is in order, though extremely difficult to formulate. On the invading presence of today's violence two viewpoints (or perhaps prejudices) have in fact been predominant; they are at first sight different from each other, but basically perhaps equivalent or convergent at least in part. I shall explain briefly.

According to the first viewpoint, which I would define as pessimistic-consolatory, there is essentially no difference between today's violence and the violence of the past. Violence is as ancient as man and the world; it has accompanied mankind throughout history. Humanity did not wait until our times to commit brutalities and heinous crimes such as torture and genocide: though the word is modern, the fact is ancient. There is, therefore, nothing new under the sun; only the external forms and instruments are different. Could one declare Genghis Khan to have been better than Stalin, or at least less violent, because he used artisans' instruments? Only two things make today's violence appear new—oblivion and illusion.

Let's first consider *oblivion*. Time, in its radical ambivalence, offers advantages and disadvantages. If, on one hand, its unceasing flow points to the vanishing of all life, on the other, it wipes suffering out of our memory: a moment of happiness and peace is enough to obliterate all suffering. In his tenacious will to live, man usually remembers his successes and his achievements clearly, but only confusedly his bitterness and his defeats. Therefore, we tend to minimize and to forget easily the violences of the past— after all they were suffered by others; for us they are only fading images or indirect representations—while we allow ourselves to be impressed and stricken by today's violence, which assaults both our flesh and spirit.

What about *illusion?* Modern man was convinced that he had definitely outgrown violence through civilization and progress and that he had relegated it to a past that, with the elapsing of time, appeared farther and farther away. Violence was an attribute of "primitive men," of "barbarians," of the dark age; it has been fading away as "enlightenment," urban civilization, and scientific and industrial development prevail over superstition, peasant civilization, and military society. The certainty of this victory grows and assumes a definite meaning with the Enlightenment thinkers and the early and present-day positivists: from Voltaire to Saint-Simon and Comte, from Spencer to Russell. In reality, violence has not been outgrown, but merely masked by "good manners," politeness. If the illusion is persistent—which is why today's violence seems an astounding novelty—the screen imposed upon it is fragile; therefore violence breaks it whenever it wishes. It is necessary to abandon the illusion and take cognizance, clearly and coldly, of an unmodifiable reality.

In this perspective, aside from oblivion and illusion, violence presents itself as man's insuperable *destiny,* which we must acknowledge without yielding to excessive fears or to illusory hopes. Perhaps no one emphasized with the radicalism of Nietzsche this destiny of violence in all its forms: from brutality to plebeian vulgarity, from massive physical imposition to subtle but no less coercive conformism. His was doubtless a violence not transcended, but transfigured in the will to power of the superman. On the other hand, Freud, though not reaching Nietzsche's radicalism, is nevertheless peremptory: "There is no hope in the attempt to suppress man's aggressive tendencies," he wrote in his well-known answer to Einstein.[2]

This viewpoint is pessimistic in the extreme in some of its formulations. Not only can we not free ourselves from violence, since it is inseparable from the human condition, but violence, as pure natural fact, appears to be nonjudicable: it is an event only to suffer and to record. On the other hand, this assessment gives consoling results without paradox, though they are as skeptical in tone as any intellectualistic pessimism.[3] There is, in fact, no particular reason to complain about present-day violence, since our predecessors shared the same destiny, just as our successors will do. The expectation remains that, in the natural alternation of things, this violence will vanish and be replaced by an interim of tranquility.

The second viewpoint, which I call apocalyptical-soteriological, holds, on the contrary, that today's violence is entirely new. And that certainly is not because the forms and instruments of contemporary violence (being undoubtedly new) are considered to be superior. It is true that between Machiavelli's *The Prince* and the numerous present-day manuals for urban or peasant guerrilla warfare there is an immense gap and that the technical superiority of contemporary guerrilla warfare is indisputable insofar as tactical training in the use of violence is concerned. The question, however, is not of technical novelty, methods, and instruments, but of the novel meaning that violence assumes. Such a meaning, however, in no way implies the minimizing of the earlier violence whose aggressive presence characterizes history. On the contrary, according to the second viewpoint, all is violence more generally than in the first viewpoint, since all past particular and contingent violences have grown to create, in a manner of speaking, a situation of global violence. All the limited contradictions of the past

2. Freud, "Warum Krieg?" [Why war?], in *Il disagio della civiltà e altri saggi* (Turin, 1971), p. 295.

3. Which, being precisely intellectualistic, avoids translating itself into the praxis resulting from it: suicide.

relative to this or that country, to this or that culture, to this or that class, issued forth in total contradiction and, therefore, in absolute and intolerable violence. This makes all of history nothing but a contradiction, a violence without counterpart—neither redeemed nor redeemable by enlightenment or progress. Reaching its maturity, humanity found itself at a dead end from which it cannot escape without blasting away the barriers. One cannot free oneself from violence without doing violence to history by ceasing to be subjected to it and by reconstructing it anew. But to do this requires an absolute violence that would make a *tabula rasa* of all crystallized past violences, of all history. Herein is found the apocalyptical sense that confers novelty on contemporary violence, which is not an end in itself, not an uncontrolled manifestation of an inescapable anthropological destiny. Rather, it has a conscious goal, which is to open a new destiny: it is no longer, as in the past, an endured, and therefore meaningless violence, but violence consciously sought.

From this perspective—which aims at a demystifying lucidity while it is simply Manichean—today's violence is a Janus. Having on the one hand immersed the past into a dark hell of errors, impositions, contradictions, and brutality, it assaults such a past with a destructive and total fury; on the other hand, it leads to a future that would no longer know either violence or struggle— the future of man's total liberation. The character Kirilov of *The Devils*, in what is perhaps Dostoevsky's most prophetic passage, and Trotsky's idea of revolutionary action (praxis and theory) in the reality of history express this vision in the most exemplary and exhaustive manner, certainly better than do their intellectualistic, repetitive imitators like Merleau-Ponty or Sartre, to say nothing of the most recent ones. We are, then, facing a liberating violence, which gives not only a political or social or economic liberation but a more profound and global one. The liberation from a false destiny, now reduced to a mere historical sedimentation, presents itself therefore as an anthropological liberation. From an epochal and absolute violence emerges the new man, free of any bond, finally master of himself.

The two views, while disagreeing in their assessment of the

importance and frequency of today's violence, do agree on one very important point: that of attributing to violence in general the role, at times prevalent, at times absolute, of protagonist in the drama of history. The agreement is significant, above all if we consider the political types that exemplify those points of view: the *Realpolitiker* (the first) and the revolutionary (the second). Irreconcilable enemies on the level of praxis, they are united to their depths in their common acceptance of and familiarity with violence.

I shall try later to examine the various reasons for this common acceptance. For the time being I shall confine myself to observing that each of the two opposite theses radicalizes the problem of world violence according to a unilateral perspective. Thus, violence will not be in a position to have an antagonist worthy of the name (and of violence itself). According to the first viewpoint, in fact, reason and virtue, when not held to be deceitful (as Nietzsche claimed they were) are subordinated to violence, since at best they help to tolerate its fatality, not to judge and transcend it. Between violence and its opposite there is, therefore, neither authentic antinomy nor dialectics, but simply a naturalistic alternation against which man is powerless. According to the second viewpoint, violence finds nothing that lowers its frequency or effectively opposes it as long as its historical time of (fatal) domination lasts. Only a radical break in the fabric of history can cause it to stop and (again fatally) to stop forever, with the advent of a new time and a new man. Not even in this case is there either authentic antinomy or dialectics: violence and nonviolence are, in fact, placed in two chronological moments clearly separated from each other, both completely uniform but with opposite tendencies.

Such an adialectical unilaterality is doubtless faulty, it seems to me, because it ends either in moral skepticism (in the case of the first viewpoint) or in abstract fideism (in the case of the second), thus revealing itself to be fallacious. On one side, violence is not simply a nonjudicable destiny only to be tolerated but, due to its constant potential for reemergence, a type of action to be evaluated and rejected on the basis of a superior principle. On the other side, it is absurd to think of humanity as being first violent and then peaceful. This would mean either to eliminate from the past every peaceful feeling (which would deprive us of a necessary point of view to identify and define violence) or to reduce it to pure and inoperative ideality, that is, fantasy. As we cannot control our dreams (much less materialize them), so in the past completely unrealizable peaceful dreams arose unconsciously. How, then, can we make nonviolence alone dominant tomorrow without preventing its opposite—violence? Is it not a question, even in this case, of a consolatory fantasizing, of a rosy dream?

In truth, between these two viewpoints that are opposed and yet in part converging, a third was formulated, which could be defined as optimistic-activistic. According to this principle, today's violence is greater than that of the past, but in substance the violence boils down to a crisis of transformation. Every period of profound change in the social setup brings about intensive and distressing upheavals in customs, feelings, consolidated ways of thinking, acceptance of ethical and social values. The old points of reference have vanished; the new are not yet generally understood and accepted. The result is a psychological and behavioral imbalance and, above all, that disorientation aptly defined by Émile Durkheim as *anomie*, that leaves ample room for the impulsiveness of violence. Our epoch is undergoing a more intense and rapid transformation than history has known—at least the history of which we are conscious—because of the advent of a technological civilization that has launched us beyond this earth—the toilsome earth of the peasant and the human planet earth as well.[4] No wonder, then, that unusual violence arises—the violence of the disoriented or of the nostalgic, who grudge change, but also, as the pacifist Comte already admitted, of those who will not let antihistorical emotive reactions stop or change the course of progress. This would be, however, like the natural though painful travail of giving birth, which is bound to come to an end. And the end of violence will come much faster if one advances more

4. On this see my books *La sfida tecnologica*, 4th ed. (Bologna, 1971); and *L'uomo tolemaico* (Milan, 1975).

decisively and rapidly toward the completion of the new social order and the education to the new image of man and his world. It is easy to understand that this viewpoint has a more sophisticated vision than does the old doctrine of progress, whose rationalistic optimism and operative activism remain, however, unchallenged.

Can this viewpoint be called more satisfactory than the two others? I do not think so. On one hand, it actually unilaterally reduces violence to mere reaction (by clumsy old fogies or fragile, unbalanced elements) to a self-confident progress that is sure of its "magnificent destiny" and that discards or denies fideistically the possibility of failures, deviations, or regressions in the human adventure. And history does not fail to provide indisputable examples of "courses and recourses," of alternations between "greatness and decadence," of "challenges" left unanswered, to use the terms of Vico, Montesquieu, and Arnold Toynbee. On the other hand, the third viewpoint shows itself to be incapable of grasping either the messianic substratum of so much of current violence or the violent aspects and results that reveal themselves to be intrinsic to or involved in many ideas and practices considered, rashly and optimistically, to be thoroughly progressive.

To conclude, we must say that all these points of view in one way or another seem to suffer from the error of unilaterality and abstractness, proving themselves inadequate. It appears more realistic (in history as well as in personal experience) to recognize that if violence is a concrete possibility never to be completely eliminated from existence, it is neither the dominant characteristic synthesizing the human nor the cure for violence itself. Ontological reflection on the dual human structure points to other answers to violence; and if we wish to understand it clearly, this structure implies the psychoanalytical dialectics of *eros* and *thanatos* [death], of aggregation and aggressiveness. On the other hand, any unilateral point of view negatively conditions the careful observation of the phenomenon and prejudices the objective analysis necessary to understand and evaluate contemporary violence.

The novelties

If my rejection of the current viewpoints (because of their unilaterality) has allowed me to clear the ground from prejudices which might have misled the analysis, the question of today's violence still remains to be tackled. In fact, it is yet to be formulated in precise terms. I perceive in this respect two sets of problems.

First, although violence is either a possibility, a moment, or a temptation (depending on the language used) constantly present in human existence, does today's violence assume new aspects or not? And if so, what are they? Second, if not all is violence in man, then can one draw the limits of violence and define it precisely? And why did it today cross its boundaries to emerge (in the opinion of many) as an all-encompassing characteristic of existence, at least of the present historical epoch? As we can see, the last question brings us back to the first set of problems, on which we must dwell in a preliminary way.[5] Moreover, although it is subordinate to the first within the domain of logic, it is nevertheless the one which presents itself most urgently to our immediate consciousness.

To put it in more precise terms: is there something new or even peculiar in today's violence, beyond the "progress" of its forms and techniques and aside from its finalistic sense? I would say yes. Its novelty is encountered along two lines: in the way it is perceived and in the way it is evaluated.

A

Let us consider the first general aspect of its novelty. We can observe here three principal modes in the perception of violence.

First, the perception of its spatial diffusion and its omnipresence. Man's planetary space is today *continuous* and *inseparable*, because everything in it is contiguous and communicating. It is not interrupted by unknown and mysterious zones in which one

5. I shall begin to deal with the second set of problems in chapter 3.

can confine, with consolatory and hopeful imagination, either the frightening brutality or the "happy islands"[6] of perfect peace and harmony. In this space of intensive communication, information and messages of violence arrive from everywhere and circulate constantly. These surely do not reflect all the actual truth, but, due to the dominance in our times of the new audiovisual language,[7] it is violence that makes the news. Not only because of the sour (and sometimes masochistic) taste for the exciting, but primarily because of the inveterate habit (or ontological reaction?) of considering it to be a hurtful and deprecable, abnormal event.

Therefore, to the extent that today's human space is unified (and manipulated or camouflaged) by the news, not only is the dream of perfect happiness suppressed but peaceful behavior loses its relevance. Who cares about knowing that in such and such a country government officials or judges are not killed, trains are not blown up, people are not taken hostage, or families are not practicing incest? All this is commonplace and accepted, but paradoxically (because it is not divulged) it comes to the point of seeming sporadic and unmotivated, whereas violence appears as the norm rather than the exception. Only excessively brutal violence becomes exceptional. The consciousness (founded or unfounded) of the universality of violence therefore spreads like an endemic disease that is difficult to stem. In this representation there is no human group, nation, or continent that is not immersed in violence. Doubtless this representation of ubiquitous violence elsewhere (but where is *elsewhere* in continuous space?) favors the consciousness that here, too, *in our home* (and where are the boundaries of *our home* in continuous space?) there is nothing but violence.

Second, the perception of the concentration of violence in time. In the world of news, "whose time is *rush*," to paraphrase

6. It is known that the typical seat of utopias is an island, because isolation is the condition of their thinkableness.

7. Such language, it is to be noted, is in itself violent, because the immediacy with which it strikes allows no time for reflection, while stimulating emotivity.

Nietzsche,[8] it is even disputable whether one can distinguish the influence of time from that of space. We live rather in a contracted spatiotemporal dimension, in which synchrony and diachrony converge and pervade each other in a reciprocal feedback.[9] Therefore, in the rapid influx of messages of violence from everywhere, our time (not only the historical epoch in which we live, but the very consciousness of time) presents itself as violence-time. The immediacy of news—which, as I said, features violence—in fact occupies our time solidly, and every moment of calm reflection is set aside if not driven away.

In this case, too, there is a paradox. The duration (external or internal, solidified in or by institutions or etched into our consciousness by memory) that we were accustomed to think of as characteristic of normalcy—the normalcy that extends undisturbed and regular in time—is now assimilated, almost bound, by that which first appeared as occasional and exceptional. It is violence in its globality that now appears as if it is of major total duration and beyond the discontinuity of the time of single acts in which it expresses itself. The violence that accelerated time exerts on our consciousness, upsetting its internal rhythms of duration and therefore its perception and judgment, corresponds (due to the intensity of the news of violence) to the current period of violence. Space and time, then, violent today as never before when space—not entirely explored and therefore not contiguous—and time—extended and lasting and not accelerated and contracted in the immediate consciousness—left gaps or confined violence to the contingency of its moments and the exceptionality of its occurrences.

But, one might say, all this does not correspond to fact; it is only a sensation, a superimposed image of the world that, under the influence of mass communication, distorts reality unilaterally. And one should not be subjected to such sensations or images, but should interpret them and reduce them to their function as

8. Nietzsche, *Al di là del bene e del male* aphorism 213, (Milan, 1968), p. 122.
9. On this see my *La sfida tecnologica*, pp. 67–74.

instruments for information; they certainly must not be considered to be elements conditioning our knowledge. But aside from the difficulty of breaking the net of messages that surrounds us, the fact is that the sensation of an omnipresent and continuous violence determines (or is determined by? I will discuss this later) a state of mind more complex and less immediate and, therefore, finally more influential.

The third aspect of violence to be considered is the extension of its field. The number of violent events continually perceived brings about, sooner or later, the loss of its precise meaning. Violence no longer appears to be a well-defined type of activity itself, but to be inherent in any act or activity, so that "all is (perceived as) violence." This perception exerts itself in two directions, the first of which concerns the present. In the past not every harmful or injurious or unjust act was defined as violent. One need merely open a penal code to notice that, in its precise and calculated taxonomy, it classifies only specific illicit acts as violence. And in this the codes reflect common judgment; they are fully agreed upon by professional criminals and by experts in normative regulations who are cautious not to go beyond certain limits. Unlawful acts committed with skill and cunning were never thought of as acts of violence. In order to classify them as violent, it was necessary that their unlawfulness be permeated with brutality. Similarly, on the level of international relations not every war was considered to be violent, but only those wars that were unjustified, that broke out suddenly, and that were cruel beyond limits.

Nowadays, on the contrary, the distinctions seem to have disappeared and violence is seen in every unjust act or instance of wrong behavior, and even in acts and behavior once deemed to be dutiful. The concern of parents for their children, if it is even slightly exaggerated—and even if it is only a bit persistent—is immediately characterized as violence, and so also is any slight severity in discipline or study at school. It is unnecessary to multiply examples anyone can easily find for himself.

However, it is worth noting that the attribute of violence, once limited to the *acts* (and only certain acts), is now also extended to situations in life and to institutions. Thus, we have a singular reversal: the institution, as the symbol of regularity, permanence of habits, customs, and norms, was considered to be that which excluded violence, which spread where arbitrariness and the absence of norms reigned. It is not coincidental that in Montesquieu's classification of governments, the regime of fear—despotism—is characterized by the dominance of an arbitrary will that ignores the stability of laws. Now, instead, every institution is accused of violence. Of significance is the reversal expressed by Pierre Joseph Proudhon's well-known phrase: *la propriété c'est le vol*. That which defined theft, qualifying it as illicit, was precisely the institution of property; now this not only loses its defining supremacy, identifying itself with its definition of the licit, but it is loaded with violence, all the worse as it becomes institutionalized and permanent. As for the situations of life, they are declared violent both when they have or may have a political significance, such as the workers' condition, and when they have no such significance at all, such as the urban condition in the great "technopolis" of our day.

And this is not enough: from the field of praxis (of acts and situations) violence extends—and this is its new aspect—to the theoretical field. Science, instruction, and knowledge in general are considered subtle and hidden forms of violence against the one who must learn, regardless of the use that may be made of them. I said subtle forms, but they are considered all the more penetrating and dangerous as contemporary man is reduced to his intellectualistic dimension, as envisioned by Enlightenment thinking. It is clear, in fact, that this reduction leads to the unilateral and optimistic thesis according to which the disappearance of violence is the more or less automatic outcome of the diffusion of instruction. But since this does not really occur, one is led by an equally unilateral antithesis to accuse of violence the very intellectual expressions of living.

The second direction of the field-extension of violence concerns the past and is the logical consequence of the first. If in the present all forms of existence (praxis and theory) are violent, the past could not have been otherwise. Should we perhaps opt for the conservative or reactionary heresy that laments the beautiful ancient times and judges us to be worse than our ancestors? It is more reasonable to think that historically the past is the seed of the present and finds in it its own truth. And it is, then, necessary to reinterpret all of the history of the past in terms of violence. This means all of history: not only the massacres or the wars (even if they appeared to be justified, not by imperialistic aims but by idealistic reasons such as the unification or the liberation of a nation, or the expansion of civilization), but also peace and peaceful works: from *pax romana* to *pax britannica*, from the universalization of Roman law to the superposition of a language to dialects, all is *in itself* violence, regardless of the single acts (which undoubtedly can also be violent). The *pax romana* in itself, the formation of a language in itself, were nothing but violence. Nothing of the past could escape it.

This extension in the field of violence (in the present and in the past), as we see, excludes the dialectics not only between violence and nonviolence but even between truth and error. One example will suffice to show the absurdity of such a result: an education that does not take into account the environmental culture or the personal tendencies of the pupil is faulty, but is it perhaps for this very reason that education should be considered to be an error or violence in itself? The error is no longer seen as a deviation or theoretical failure that becomes corrigible; but it is reabsorbed into the practical category of violence, where there is no point in trying to distinguish it from truth. The relevance of the subjective intention disappears, and with it the objective relevance, the meaning itself of the acts, behavior, and precise facts: the only sense is given by all-encompassing violence, like the night where all cows look black.

B

The three extensions of violence (in space, time, and field) at which we have arrived today seem to validate the apocalyptical point of view. Without yet discussing the merit of that interpretation, I confine myself for the moment to observing only that the novelty lies in the subjective sensitivity to violence rather than in its increased objective and actual presence. But this is of no small importance: in substance the point of view that violence (or at least its diffusion and influence) is everywhere and that everything is violence depends in large measure on a subjective attitude, on the sensation and conviction of being more immersed in violence, more dominated by it, than we were or believe we were in the past. It is in reference to this state of mind that the other aspect of novelty—the evaluative—acquires its highest importance.

The truly characteristic development in our times is in fact the *exaltation* of violence. However diligently one may search in the history of thought up until the nineteenth century, there is no consistent trace of such exaltation to be found. Violence could be (and was) recognized as inevitable, as something to be subjected to without hope of ever eliminating it, but it was certainly not appreciated. It was considered to be an evil, the evil often lying at man's root: *hubris*, the excess, the arrogance of those who hold themselves apart from and above all law and harmony in life.[10] And if at times people were taught how to use violence, it was because in some circumstances it was thought to be a necessary evil, certainly not a good. Even Machiavelli shared this view. It is true that in the past one may find numerous exaltations of force: Simone Weil wrote a penetrating analysis in her *Iliade, poème de la force*.[11] However, that poem is not an exaltation but a registration of the uplifting yet frightening (therefore, dialectical) presence of force; in any case, whatever Weil might have thought (her terminology in this respect is uncertain), the question there was of force, not violence. This distinction is one to which I must return, since recently it has been for the most part lost and every use of force has been identified with violence. This was not so in the past. It is enough to think of the well-known cases of Callicles and Thrasymachus, whose praises of force fall into contradiction when Socrates leads them to face real violence. The predominance

10. See C. del Grande, *Hybris* (Naples, 1947); and also A. Camus, *L'homme révolté* (Paris, 1951), p. 44ff.

11. It is one of the essays in Weil's *La Grecia e le intuizioni precristiane* (Turin, 1967).

of force is, for Socrates' two interlocutors, a law of nature; that of violence is not.

This ancient and secular condemnation of violence nowadays seems to be largely disregarded. Some citations will suffice to prove the point. Lenin, in remembering the famous "panegyric" of violence by Engels in *Antidühring*, proclaims "the necessity for systematically educating the masses in *this* . . . conception of violent revolution."[12] He is echoed in the thirties by the *Union de lutte des intellectuels révolutionnaires* (generally of surrealistic inspiration) with its incitement to "violence," to "fanaticism," to "death penalty," to the "physical destruction of the servants of capitalism."[13] If Mao Tse-tung asserts that "power stems from a gun barrel," Sartre expands (in his preface to *Les Damnes de la terre* by Fanon): "The weapon of a fighting man is his humanity," and Merleau-Ponty pushes the assertion to the limit: "History is terror because there is in it a contingency . . .; violence is our world since we are made of flesh."[14]

This current exaltation (of which we could multiply the citations endlessly) becomes clear from what I have said in the preceding pages. In fact, if we have violence in *everything* and *everywhere*, we have one, and only one choice: either to suffer it with resignation (in which case violence appears to be the supreme law of life, man's destiny) or to try to eliminate it. But if we choose the second, we become prisoners of an all-encompassing premise: in order to eliminate violence it is necessary to make use of it, since there is no other means for antiviolent action. Such action, therefore, will not renounce the *materiality* of violence, but will reverse its direction: something destructive will be rendered constructive in the hope that through this reversal it will be neutralized and will disappear.[15] By virtue of its new direction, violence becomes,

12. Lenin, *Stato e rivoluzione*, chap. 1, sec. 4 (Rome, 1963), p. 24.

13. "Contre-Attaque" (1935), now in A. Breton, *La position politique du surréalisme* (1972), pp. 175–77.

14. Merleau-Ponty, *Humanisme et terreur* (Paris, 1974), pp. 98, 118.

15. This is what Merleau-Ponty emphasizes, ibid., pp. 104–5.

to use Sartre's icastic image, "Achilles' spear," which wounds and heals at the same time.

On the other hand, violent action against violence will never, given the premise, be anything but total. It must fill all space (thus becoming universal) and time, which is possible only by re-jecting the entire past. It must, that is, make the original speci-mens of men into sons of themselves.[16] All the institutions and ethical and cultural suprastructures must be eliminated in order to open the way toward complete spontaneousness. The human uni-verse, synthesized by violence, implies therefore a rigorously logical idea of revolution.

The observation is banal, so evident is the connection between revolution and violence; however, it calls for some brief com-ment. It would, for example, be important to investigate if, from the point of view of the history of ideas, it was the advent of the idea of revolution that brought about the conviction of the all-encompassing meaning of violence, or whether the contrary is true. But this is not the point. As we know, the term "revolution" no longer carries its ancient meaning—which was drawn from as-tronomy and was related to the idea of cyclicity—of a return to the beginnings (and to the principles) in order to start anew the human itinerary. In the modern sense it denotes, instead, a *com-pletely* new beginning, without antecedents, as must be made after an earthquake completely wipes out old buildings. But in the modern sense of revolution, the "earthquake" is deliberately brought about, willed as a "liberation" that is a supreme hope transformed into a concrete activity and aimed at the realization of the absolute values of man. It is precisely this thoroughly positive conception of revolution as hope (the "hope of the revolution," to use the happy expression by Vittorio Mathieu) that legitimizes violence and permits the exaltation of it.

Its correlation with the idea of revolution and of "new begin-

16. To the decisive idea of "self-birth" in Marx (see *Opere filo-sofiche giovanili* [Rome, 1950], p. 235) B. Romano has acutely called attention in his *La liberazione politica* (Ancona, 1976), pp. 46ff.

ning" explains why violence was able to prevail so widely during these last years over the opposite ideal of nonviolence, which seemed destined to worldwide success in the wake of Gandhi.[17] But violence succeeded even in making nonviolence its own instrument. In fact, the nonviolent techniques are now reversed from their proper sense and utilized for the tactics of a more crafty and effective struggle than the open one, since "the capacity of oppressors to commit violence will always be immeasurably greater than that of the oppressed." Nonviolence converts itself from an expression of the revolution of love to a "strategy . . . to create conflict and aggressiveness."[18]

There is then novelty in current violence; and this novelty locates itself within the picture described by the apocalyptical viewpoint. It is not due to a change in the substance or to a different conceptual definition of violence but to a different mode of perceiving it, of assigning it a place in history and therefore evaluating it. It is legitimate, then, to suspect that it is not violence that has changed, but we ourselves; but this escapes those who hold the apocalyptical viewpoint. Perhaps the exaltation of violence— a very recent phenomenon, I repeat—is the result of very ambitious but too often frustrating hopes. This issue I shall now try to explore.

17. Fanon-Sartre's model of decolonization through violence seems, in fact, to have completely replaced Gandhi's nonviolent model.

18. I draw the quoted phrases (which belong to J. M. Muller, *Il significato della nonviolenza*) from B. Montanari, *Obiezione di coscienza* (Milan, 1976), pp. 157–58, where there are lucid considerations on the topic.

Chapter 2
Course and recourse of violence

The antiviolent course

In the history of Western violence (to confine myself to the modern or postmedieval) one can trace, if only in broad lines, a cycle of the Vichean type: a (slow) "course" and a (rapid) "recourse." In the course, one observes the conscious and precise effort to restrain and overcome violence, which presupposes the traditional negative judgment on it. In the recourse one observes, instead, the phenomenon of all-inclusiveness and appreciation of violence, which I referred to in the preceding chapter: violence returns like a high tide to reclaim the (theoretical and practical) territory from which it was thought to have been forced to withdraw. And it returns not as a result of a natural cause, as a sort of mechanical alternation, but because it is deliberately invited.

Let us try to outline the main aspects of the course. It is impossible here to mark every step of it; suffice it to say that the whole process of formation and affirmation of the modern, sovereign, and unitary state (the postimperial) was interpreted as the overcoming of disorder and violence by the accompanying cul-

ture, which motivates or justifies the process. This is the interpretation offered at the beginning of the modern state by both the
theorists of the *tiers parti* (the *politiques*) of the time of the French
religious wars and by Hobbes and Spinoza above all; even Des-
cartes, despite his aloofness from politics, subscribed to it.[1] Such
an interpretation was extended by physiocrats and Enlightenment
thinkers to encompass not only the state but also the social setup.
The peaceful and rational civilization of the Enlightenment is the
fruit of a society centered in the city (often the capital), in which
the ignorance and brutality of the peasant society[2] disappear and
the security and tranquility of civil relations, commerce, and production are established. It is above all in the Enlightenment's polemics that the new state appears to be the victor over both the
medieval feuds and factions—think of Voltaire's or Hume's reprobation of Guelphs and Ghibellines—and the violence of Renaissance power—think of the anti-Machiavellism of Voltaire or
of the young Frederick of Prussia.

But it is in the nineteenth century that this course takes on its
more precise characteristics, those which show the sure triumph
over violence. This assertion may be astonishing, so much is that
century marked by wars and revolutions and by theories in which
war (Clausewitz, Hegel), revolution (Mazzini, Marx, Bakunin, to
recall only the founders of the three revolutionary "holy families"), and power politics (Treitschke) are given a positive or at
least realistic interpretation. Certainly, the openly pacifist doctrines and movements, though present in that century, are not
those that seem to prevail through their theoretical vigor and their
direct and practical influence on the reality (not at all peaceful) of
nineteenth-century praxis and theory. And yet it is the pacifists'
outlooks and aims that in the end impress upon that praxis and
theory a meaning contrary to violence. Clausewitz is a theorist of

1. See A. Del Noce, *Riforma cattolica e filosofia moderna, I: Cartesio*
(Bologna, 1965), pp. 537–79.
2. The physiocratic preference for agriculture should not mislead
us: it is not at all the defense of "peasant" civilization, but the proposal for a landowners' society, rationalized and productive.

war, not an advocate of it, and so is Hegel;[3] Mazzini, Marx, and Bakunin—though hostile to one another—are theorists of a revolution that has a precise aim and purpose; they do not think at all of a "permanent" revolution; Treitschke condemns a power that does not serve the highest ideals of humanity.[4]

The fact is that the nineteenth century draws its optimistic and confident perspective precisely from its own realistic-activistic currents of thought. Its great secular faiths—historicism, positivism, Marxism, evolutionism—find inspiration, in various ways, in the idea of progress (be it gradual or by fits and starts) and in its pacifying capability, and they come to the final conclusion that violence will be overcome. It is not coincidental that at the dawn of the new century Vladimir Solovyov makes a character who represents the idea of progress—"the political man"[5]—express this conviction demonstrated by nineteenth-century civilization.

Setting aside the theories, I will try to demonstrate along which lines and in which concrete respects the decline of nineteenth-century violence was achieved. I shall examine three key sectors: civil relations, political relations, and international war relations.

CIVIL RELATIONS

In fact, both the creation and the strengthening of a central organization of the state, which secures the monopoly of force, and the technical evolution of weapons (through concentrated and expensive industrial production) upset the balance of power in favor of public force. Banditry and private violence are in general clearly inferior to public power and become, therefore, exceptional cases or strictly personal cases, losing their previous endemic mass-character. One may think of the frequent extortions on highways

3. See C. Cesa, *Hegel filosofo politico* (Naples, 1976), pp. 171–201.
4. Cf. his criticism of Machiavelli in *Politik* 1:89–91 and 2:54 (Leipzig, 1897).
5. In *Tre dialoghi sulla guerra, il progresso e la fine della storia universale* (Turin, 1975), pp. 138–40. The personal view of Solovyov is known to be different.

or country roads, of the dangers in blind alleys or suburban areas: these are phenomena that in the nineteenth century tended to disappear rapidly. Thanks to its organizational and material superiority, "public force" saw the necessity of the use of force to be much reduced, the prestige or the threat of power being generally sufficient for maintaining order. Banditry survives only where public organization has not yet arrived or is weak, or, as Hannah Arendt[6] justly emphasized, where the state is in decay. In short, public force is the counterpart of private violence: where the former asserts itself, the latter loses ground and tends to disappear.

However, the question involves not only facts or concrete expressions of force, but principles as well. What in the nineteenth century disappeared even more than private material power is the idea itself of *private justice*. Private justice, being tied to the particularism of a class-structured state, to the institutionalized plurality of its social stratifications and, therefore, to the merger of public and private interests, is constantly prone to "taking justice into its own hands." Duels, vengeances, and abuses of power are the negative sides of class *honor*, in which Montesquieu clearly perceived the "principle" of the class-based state. In the nineteenth century this idea was dethroned by the opposite idea, which advocates a *public* justice administering a law understood as the expression of the will of the state, as "a general will," to use Rousseau's celebrated formula. The possibility that private justice is, or appears to be, violent for those who suffer it is therefore rejected at its root by a common and public justice. This is one of the most relevant results of the magnificent transformation from the private-oriented state to the public-oriented state.

In short, to the extent that the state (the state bounded by law) in the nineteenth century assumed a unitary and rigorously public organization having the monopoly not only on force but also on the administration of justice and subordinated its organization to a general law, it proportionately eliminated violence from the mind before it materialized into fact.

6. Arendt, *Sulla violenza* (Milan, 1971), pp. 60–62.

POLITICAL RELATIONS

It is unnecessary to emphasize that with the introduction of the parliamentary-representative system on the institutional level and compulsory education on the social level the nineteenth-century state decisively embarked on the road to an approved and shared authority. The critical and difficult question was no longer whether there should be representation and participation, but *how much* there should be. In light of this question, the work initiated by the absolute monarchy takes on a new meaning, as it was aimed at eliminating the possibility of internal political conflicts brought about by the rivalry of the various feudal or social powers. That which the English called the "king's peace" was transformed into the community's public order, which was founded on active consensus, the delegation of authority, and control on government leaders, and no longer on the charismatic prestige of the monarch and on his dominant material power. The nineteenth-century activity had, therefore, a broader scope: it tended to liberate power from its authoritarianism and to base it on liberty and rationality.[7] On principle, then, violence ceased to be one of the normal instruments of internal politics, since its possibility was no longer inherent in the very structure of the state.

But there is a more significant point. Despite the above-mentioned state transformation, the nineteenth century was the period of great and frequent insurrections, of powerful political movements that waved the flag of revolution in the name of the still-unattained conversion of power to reason and freedom. Indeed, it is in this very sector that we witness a significant retrogression of the idea of violence. Before pointing out the lines of such retrogression, however, it is necessary to glance back briefly.

The modern age has already marked—with the first English Puritan Revolution of 1640[8]—an important structural change in insurrectional violence: the passage from revolt to revolution.

7. Some good observations are found in J. Habermas, *Storia e critica dell' opinione pubblica* (Bari, 1971), pp. 102–3.
8. The second, that of 1688, has nothing but the name of revolu-

Previous history had known numberless *revolts*—of slaves against masters, of peasants against landowners, of serfs against feudal lords, of poor against rich, of subjects against aristocratic or bourgeois oligarchies (think of Geneva), and so on—but had experienced no revolution in the proper sense. Revolt and revolution are ideal types of action, each very different from the other in structure and phenomenological meaning. Since I have dealt with the problem elsewhere,[9] I shall confine myself to a few essential observations. Revolt is a popular movement that for the most part originates spontaneously; it is generally provoked by an intolerable situation of poverty and/or servitude and appears to be the consequence of a perceived degeneration of mythicized good times of old and even of a legendary primitive golden age. It has neither a definite sociopolitical program, since the reference to the past is enough, nor an organization or rational strategy. Revolution, on the contrary, has a general objective and a constructive sociopolitical program addressed to the future (even if the myth of the origins may be present in it in a more or less unconscious manner); therefore, it creates an ideological-praxistic organization, which elaborates and directs its political-military strategy. Consider the New Model Army of the English Puritan Revolution, the clubs and secret societies of the French Revolution, the Leninist militia-party, and the Long-March army of Mao Tsetung. It will suffice to compare the (peasant) *revolt* of Pugachev with the (urban) October *Revolution* to see the difference. There is no doubt that violence—at the center of both types of action and in both subjectively legitimized by an aspiration to justice—nevertheless takes on very different configurations. While in a revolt it is passional, tumultuous, unstable, and uncontrolled (an

---

tion because of the scruple of legality that inspired it and the use, more ostentatious than real, of arms.

9. In my article "Rivoluzione e rivolta" in *Proteus* (1970) 1: 3–10, and in *L'uomo tolemaico* (Milan, 1975), pp. 84–97. On this topic see a more detailed analysis by J. Ellul, *Autopsia della rivoluzione* (Turin, 1974), chap. 1.

Enlightenment thinker would call it backward because of its peasant origin), in a revolution it is disciplined, organized, and calculated (progressive because of its urban origin)—at least in design
and general strategy, since it is evident that in the complex revolutionary vicissitudes the most ardent moments escape a complete
discipline because of their contingency: as in a war, spontaneousness has free play. In short, in a revolt, violence, conscious or not,
dominates. In a revolution, on the contrary, violence is an *instrument* and like all instruments is subject to the art of using it; thus
not every act of violence is required and justified, but only those
that are homogeneous and are clearly tools in the revolutionary
design. Doubtless the criterion of judgment is internal to revolution and distinguishes useful from harmful violence and not violence from nonviolence. And, moreover, it is undeniable that violence, while extending materially, with the transition from revolt
to revolution has assumed a different character from the traditional: it has become more controlled and less passional.

From this perspective, it could perhaps be said that the French
Revolution marks a step backward in relation to the English Puritan Revolution. Too many conflicting revolutionary designs
work at cross-purposes in the former, which lacks an ideological-
praxistic unity, expressing and controlling the direction of the
movement in a disciplined manner. Therefore, violence asserts its
dominating passionality in the confused conflict of ideas and currents. Indeed, Robespierre brings revolutionary design to its
highest precision and doctrinal rigor and the violence reaches its
culmination (the "Terror"), according to a process whose profound meaning no one understood as well as did Hegel in his *Phenomenology of Mind*.[10]

The different aspect of violence due to its structural change
from revolt to revolution takes on a clear-cut relevance in the
nineteenth century. It is not necessary, in order to discern it, to

10. See V. Mathieu, *La speranza nella rivoluzione* (Milan, 1972),
pp. 11–12. For a balanced critical judgment on the relations between
Hegel and the French Revolution, see C. Cesa, *Hegel, filosofo politico*,
pp. 45–81.

refer to the various openly peaceful "revolutionary" designs such as those of Robert Owen or Saint-Simon and Comte. The social change foreseen or promoted by them is doubtless radical, so that one may speak of them as *revolutionary;* but their revolution is not violent because it is brought about through education, organization, and science. The importance of these tendencies is indisputable; however, more significant, for our purpose, is the way in which Marx formulated our problem. In his formulation, revolution becomes a rigorously objective event with a scientific foundation, because it is the result of strict laws of history. It has, consequently, nothing to do either with passionality or with moral reasons (or indignation). The scorn for "virtuism" does not have its origin in Pareto but in Marx.

Doubtless in Marx the consciousness of the proletariat's misery and its historical function is very keen. But this misery, certainly not new in history, could remain powerless and find compensation in one of the various forms of "opiates of the people" as indeed has happened many times in history, if misery were not guided (in Marx's judgment) by the awareness of the laws of historical materialism. In other words, misery left to itself brings about revolts; when directed by a scientific understanding of the course of history and of its economic structure, it determines revolution.

This perspective does not invalidate the reasons for opposition between the revolutionary and the conservative, the proletarian and the capitalist, but it invalidates the motives that show this opposition to be personal in character, pregnant with emotionality that borders hatred. The capitalist (as the representative of a category) has no personal guilt; he, too, is the servant of history and, after all, a beneficial servant, particularly in relation to the proletariat, since the triumph of the former accelerates the triumph of the latter by the dialectical necessity for reversing the praxis. The Marxist revolution is, first of all, the acquired self-consciousness of the proletariat. It is well known that this tendency was accentuated by German social democracy, in which the determinism of historical materialism is pushed to the extreme, so that one can speak of a change from *revolution* to *evolution*. The capitalist-bourgeois system will crumble by itself (there is no need for insurrectional intervention) as the result of a massive and irresistible widening of the workers' presence in Parliament and in economic and social centers through the party and the union. There will be a revolution to bring about radical changes in the structure, but it will not be a violent revolution. The "midwife" of history, as Marx called it, is destined then to assist, setting aside forceps, at a painless and natural birth. In short, revolution, foreseen or determined by the law of history, disciplined in the international and national organizations of the workers' movement, transformed into evolution (Sorel would say infiltrated by the bourgeois spirit), ceases to be the culmination of violence and becomes an impressive process of innovation, absolutely normal and peaceful. While remaining rigorously faithful to historical materialism and to its (pretended) scientific character, Marxist socialism (at least in its social-democratic orientation) comes to join at the end of the century—with Marx against Marx—that form of socialism severely condemned by Marx as "utopistic" and humanitarian.

WAR RELATIONS

The third aspect to be considered in the field of international relations is the nineteenth-century war discipline illustrated by compliance with the laws of war.

Over the centuries war has found itself in an ambiguous and ill-defined position, oscillating between two extremes. On the one hand, it was considered a natural and fateful event, exempt from any regulation that did not further the political interest or the interest of its own *art*, whose aim was victory. Think of Hannibal and Caesar, the great classical masters, or of Machiavelli's *Art of War*. War was then a humanized event, because it was disciplined by intelligence according to the means-to-an-end relationship, but certainly not because it was subject to judgment and moral determination. On the other hand, it was held subordinate to moral laws and, therefore, to the judicial norms of natural law. Think of the philosophical formulations of Saint Augustine and Saint Thomas or of the harsh condemnation by Dante of the stratagem of Guido da Montefeltro: "Promise great things; promise, and do not pay" [*Inferno*, XXVII, 110].

Between these two opposite positions, the scale was tipping to the side of the first under the weight of the reality of both political interest at play (and for politics, war is the decisive game) and the violence unleashed in armed confrontation. Some examples will clarify the point. The Middle Ages, it is true, had made an effort to bring war within the norms of a chivalric code founded on the principle of honor.[11] Nevertheless, in a sense, Philippe de Commines already viewed these rules with detachment and irony and wondered whether the given word should be kept even against the interest of the state. In another sense, the chivalric norms were not sufficient to check violence against the people or against those who, because they were not noble, could not be ransomed with payment in gold. Not without reason, therefore, could Ariosto smile at the "great goodness of ancient knights" as at an idyllic fable contrasting with the hard reality of war. Likewise, in the modern age, while the rigorous and precise development of a scientific theory of *ius belli* [the law of war] is to be credited to the theology of war and above all to the Spanish school from Vitoria to Suarez, the remembrance of the horrors of war, represented by the realistic engravings of Callot or in some of the ironic and bitter pages of Voltaire's *Candide*, is sufficient to allow us to measure the abysmal gap between theory and praxis.

The nineteenth century proposes to fill this gap by bringing praxis and theory closer together. The times are particularly difficult. In principle, the formation of the state, not only sovereign but also national (sacred!), makes war a logical and normal fact, both because of the rejection of a superior divine or natural law (the state is now the source of the law) and because of the exaltation of the national character of culture. War appears, indeed, as politics carried out by nonpolitical means. On material grounds, this is the moment in which the armies (no longer seignorial and therefore temporary) cease to be mercenary; they expand into the

11. See the enlightening pages by J. Huizinga, *L'autunno del Medio Evo* (Florence, 1966).

"armed nation" and strengthen themselves with ideological[12] motives and more powerful and deadly weapons.

And it is in this historical situation, in which the war phenomenon finds (or seems to find) its full justification as well as the primary reasons for its development toward a total war,[13] that nineteenth-century civilization senses the possible risk of the unlimited expansion of violence implied in modern war. One might say that it tried to avert its own negative possibility, counterbalancing it with the effort to humanize war, bringing it within the boundaries of law. This effort, in fact, was translated into precise juridical norms,[14] such as respect for civilians, the wounded, and prisoners; the rights of neutrals; the institution of the International Red Cross; the prohibition of some types of weapons; the limitations of retaliation, etc. And while the *ius belli* passed from the theoretical sphere to international conventions, the institutional foundation of a *ius gentium pacis* [law of the peace of nations] began to be laid down: in the Permanent Court of Arbitration of the Hague and the International Prize Court, which are a prelude to the more organic institutions of the twentieth century.

On the other hand, the replacement of the so-called military society by the industrial society made it possible to hold as assured the end of war, at least as a prospect (according to Spencer, for example). By a gross logical blunder (which, however, expressed a comprehensible hope) the effect and the instrument were mistaken for the cause, and it was forgotten that the function creates the organ, the conflictive tendency the militias, and not

12. Whose potentiality for violence finds a symbolic expression and a sacral sublimation in the *Marseillaise:* "qu'un sang impur abreuve nos sillons."

13. This crucial historical point was grasped by the keen sensibility of Guglielmo Ferrero in his long-forgotten trilogy: *Aventure. Bonaparte en Italie* (Paris, 1936); *Reconstruction. Talleyrand à Vienne* (Geneva-Paris, 1940); *Pouvoir* (Paris, 1944).

14. A brief but theoretically incisive mention is found in Hegel, *Filosofia del diritto*, par. 338 and in the addition to it.

the reverse. Be that as it may, the certitude that there will be no more wars or revolutions runs through the nineteenth century despite the factual evidence to the contrary.

The peaceful and antiviolent vocation of that century, then, appears sure; it is demonstrated very clearly by the three symptomatic cases mentioned above: the decline of private violence, the disciplining of both revolution and war. In ideas, institutions, and praxis (or the direction, at least, in which praxis moved) the nineteenth century marks the highest point of the modern antiviolent course, apparently the most conscious repudiation of violence as the ineluctable and supreme destiny of man. If we want to identify the reason to which this nineteenth-century tendency owes its unity, I believe that the most likely point of reference is the "state bounded by law," in which the objective to reach the maximum of political power is associated with and mitigated by the rule of law.[15] The intent of this was to put an end to the arbitrariness of power; inside and outside, the state of law meant submission to the law: government, jurisdiction, administration, and police on the one side, foreign policy and military power on the other; all had to conform to current norms. The most effective guarantee against violence is found in the affirmation and expansion of the authority of law.

Nevertheless the course has not yet attained the goals it aimed at, so that the recourse of violence appears and grows rapidly. Let us take note of it before trying to find an explanation.

The recourse of violence

The surest way to document the recourse of violence, without pretense at completeness and with only some degree of reliability, is to observe the twentieth-century attitude toward the very key sectors in which the antiviolent tendency of the century manifested itself. From this comparison the alternation of course and recourse emerges in a symptomatic manner. However, the exami-

15. Not coincidentally, the English equivalent expression to "Stato di diritto" is "rule of law."

nation will not follow the ascending itinerary (from the private to the public to the international) that was followed to point out the decisive moments of the course. It follows, instead, a centripetal movement: from the private and the international toward the public, because here violence's rediscovery of itself as revolutionary is, in my opinion, the central and illuminating symptom of the recourse. Let us examine the facts.

THE REEMERGING OF PRIVATE VIOLENCE

In this sector, as I said above, the curb of violence was entrusted to the prevailing urban civilization in the not yet demythicized certainty of its progressive and pacifying character.[16] In truth, urban civilization is not new nor was it ever necessarily or entirely peaceful. The Greece of the golden age of the *polis*, the Middle Ages of the laborious communes, the Renaissance of the splendid cities are examples of civilizations in which the tone is established by urban life. There was no clear separation but, rather, human continuity between urban and rural life: vegetable gardens and fields crowded the city walls, which the peasants crossed with their produce according to the regular rhythm of daily life. One may recall the Siena fresco *Good Government* by Ambrogio Lorenzetti. On the other hand, among the cities' splendors and miseries, harmony and civil strife[17] stood in dialectical opposition. It is only in the nineteenth century that, theoretically, both the continuity and the internal dialectics cease: misery and brutality are ejected from the urban limits and seem destined to disappear. If in the country the candlelight does not illuminate the material and spiritual darkness, the lights of the city appear to be the material projection (and the announcement) of intellectual and moral enlightenment.

16. However, the ambivalence did not escape Balzac, torn between *la vie parisienne* and nostalgia for *la vie de province*, while Thoreau reasserted the drastic rejection pronounced by Rousseau.

17. A profound meditation on the ambivalence of the city is given by J. Ellul, *Sans feu ni lieu* (Paris, 1975).

But today, to use a symbol, urban life is at the mercy of a blackout (caused by technical accident or sabotage), which, by blocking the mechanisms and putting out the lights, seems to dissolve even the light of reason, unleashing anxiety and abuse of power, fear and aggressiveness—impulses that are removed and accumulated secretly under the polished surface of smoothly running daily habits. Paradoxically, the blackout reveals a human chaos of city life in which one is no longer in a position to live by means of one's own hands or personal resources.

Setting aside the symbol, is it true that today's city is this chaos of human relations, and why? [18] I will point out three elements.

Separation.—In the first place, there is the separation of the city into areas defined by their function: here, the directive center, public and private offices; there, the industrial and productive area; elsewhere, the residential area. On one side the night city— the dormitory; on the other the daylight city of work, in turn subdivided into areas of factories and offices. Life, therefore, runs according to fluxes that intersect like compulsory movements on a checkerboard or repeat themselves monotonously and tiresomely without freedom: from home to the workplace and from there home again. In the second place, there is the separation of professional groups or age groups: here *Du côté des Guermantes* live the rich, there the poor, elsewhere the middle class; here the parents more advanced in their careers, there the children with beginning salaries, elsewhere the elderly in economic decline. The human fabric of the city at one time was tightly woven like a tapestry— one need only read Boccaccio to realize it: beside the palace the little house; within the palace different lives, from rich to poor, from young to old; today such a fabric has vanished, fragmented along the lines of a multiple compartmentalization.

Isolation.—In the separation of places, activities, and lives there is the celebration of the sectionalization and stratification of schematized relations according to professions and activities, class, and age groups. Thus the custom (not to mention the possi-

18. I have dealt with this in my *L'uomo tolemaico*, pp. 84ff. Here I confine myself to defining the theme precisely.

bility) of free and open relations ceases, and the freedom of personal, spontaneous, and relaxed encounters ceases as well: every encounter requires a program or a specific motivation; it implies "work" even when it is not a "business meeting." The free exchange of opinions in assembly ceases; the rallies are organized, abnormal, and contingent meetings, discrete and detached from the environment: the processions of protesters are militarized marches in a foreign, if not an enemy field. A *routine* superimposes itself on another *routine* of a different sense and there is no communication between them. Assailed by so many strange, insignificant, or unbearable presences, one is pushed to segregate oneself, and so lose touch with the rhythm of surrounding life.

Artificialization.—An immense and complex artificial mechanism supports city life, indeed, makes it possible. Services (from transportation to heating) ever more unified and standardized in order to lower the cost while making life more comfortable increase the dependency of the individual and reduce the possibility of his autonomy. Thus the question of public participation is raised; why, in the private sector, are we powerless? But when the discussions of the various city committees (of district, neighborhood, apartment building) are not regimented according to a party line, they end in the futility of vain chatter or in disagreement over facts and questions of feasibility. It is fated to be so: the impossibility (and the induced incapacity) to do for oneself within a very complicated machine throws into the public domain even the most private, and therefore conflicting, demands. On the other hand, the machines lead to the imposition of other machines and complex mechanisms that regulate functioning. Overwhelmed by noises, replaced by the metallic stridency of loudspeakers, the human voice becomes inaudible, either because it is dispersed or because it is interiorized. In either case it is lost.

But separation and isolation constitute the primary conditions for the development of a continuous process that begins with incomprehension (we do not know one another, or we know one another incompletely) and develops through a schematic mythicization ("others" are always happy and powerful, or dissatisfied and hostile), prolongs itself through envy or fear, and culminates in resentment or hatred. Violence finds here the most favorable psychological conditions to sprout suddenly like the red flower of fire. When the Other is a stranger, it is easy to consider him as a purely material obstacle of which one can rid oneself without concern.

The invasive spreading of artificiality in urban life creates constant nervous tension, which in turn stimulates passional instinctuality, the desire for liberation from the suffocating weight of artifice. The brutal or desecrating gesture or words appear as a liberation from the fixity of behaviors and language. Furthermore, the artificial complexity of the urban mechanism renders it fragile, and the tight interdependence of its apparatus increases its vulnerability. On the other hand, the vertiginous development and diffusion of technology again made possible a confrontation, no more imbalanced at first, between subverters and custodians of public order. Very efficient offensive means and refined operational techniques (even financial! Think of the bands of kidnappers) are again at the disposal of private banditry. The technicalization of cities thus offers a gamut of material conditions for the new eruption of private violence (and political, but I will speak of this later).

So in a city in which the human feeling of inhabiting, conceived of as nourishing and cultivating life through interrelations, is dissolved—as was pointed out by Heidegger with much penetration[19]—separation, isolation, and artificiality are not only psychological conditions and materials favorable for violence but, through the power of suggestion, strong incitements to violence for those of both weak will and strong will for the opportunity they offer.[20] Thus, private violence is reborn and it is unnecessary to list the numerous manifestations of this we know so well: pick-

19. See the essays "Bauen, Wohnen, Denken" [Building, living, thinking] and "Dichterisch wohnt der Mensch" [Man lives poetically] in *Vorträge und Aufsätze* (Pfullingen, 1954).

20. I use, as is evident, the categories "weak and strong will" that Nietzsche uses in *Al di là del bene e del male*, aphorism 21, p. 26.

pockets, muggers, and kidnappers, rampant in city streets, are penetrating into homes. On the other hand, the disappearance of a clear imbalance in the forces of order favorable to the "guardians of order" drives them to act not only with the symbolic force of authority but with effective weapons and show of might; therefore, the conflict is rekindled and becomes bloody.

THE REEMERGING OF WAR VIOLENCE

It seems at first sight that in this sector the recourse of violence has less virulence. In fact, escalation of the power of arms to the level of the radical destructive capacity of the thermonuclear bomb had the effect of forbidding total war from the practical point of view (war using every means and being, therefore, global and spatially limitless). This is demonstrated by the stages through which the politico–military strategy has passed. I shall summarize them schematically: terror strategy (in the two successive versions of massive answer and flexible answer); dissuasive strategy; co-existence strategy.[21] The possibility of its use makes the absolute weapon (as it is called) a warning presence, which acts by threat and not by actual use; the balance or imbalance of terror seems to have the same effect as stopping the will to violence and to death. But does stopping mean dissolving violence or redirecting it to other outlets? Let us find out.

As of today, the practical impossibility of total global war is supported neither by an efficient international organization nor by a juridical supranational system that is impartial, dependable, and effective. The capacity to resolve the controversies according to justice or at least according to law is therefore lacking, to say nothing of the lack of a spirit of ecumenical solidarity and frater-nity. Lacking a measure for juridical or fraternal judgment, the

21. Let it be clear: every successive stage does not cancel but pre-serves the preceding stage, limiting itself to move it farther away to-ward the background, in which all of the stages stand out as more or less impending threats.

ideological and national tensions—superposed and intertwined so that they are difficult to distinguish—continue to intensify and press for a solution.

Among long-established countries—think of western Europe—one notices a considerable decrease in tension and a strong inclination toward interrelationship according to the nineteenth-century vision of a peaceful collaboration among distinct nationalities organized into states.[22] On the opposite side, however, one must observe the increase of conflictual tension beyond and across the boundaries (arbitrarily defined from the ethnic standpoint) of newly established independent countries.

Conflictual violence, which fortunately is prevented from leading to total and global war, has not dissolved, but has only compressed itself and therefore continues its pressure in multiple directions; it always ends by discharging itself in endemic local wars, where the terror of thermonuclear destruction no longer carries any weight; it loses its deterrent capacity because of the disproportion between the material price and the gains at stake. (But what if an uncontrolled proliferation occurred?) If it is true, then, that despite its possibility we were spared a third world war of the traditional type, it is equally true that we are experimenting with a new type of war. From 1945 until today the world has had no peace even for a year. An unacknowledged multiple war, splintered and spread out over space and time, conducted with conventional but nevertheless extremely destructive weapons, has kept alive everywhere the embers of violence that are the armed conflicts. The still incomplete measure of material and human losses and of the suffering caused by these partial conflicts is certainly higher than that of the past world wars. In any case, these were, as Heidegger understood it, only "the preliminary form that takes on the suppression of the difference between peace and war," the announcement of a new state of affairs "in which the element

22. Perhaps for more empirical reasons than those romantically indicated at the time: the necessity for exchanges and wider markets, productive concentrations, mobility of labor and capital, military security, etc.

'war' will not be felt as such and the element 'peace' will no longer have any meaning or substance."[23]

We should not forget, moreover, that with few exceptions local wars are not possible without international cooperation from allies that, on the one hand, supply the modern, costly war materials and the very necessary diplomatic and propaganda support and that, on the other, prevent local wars from reaching the thermonuclear level. In the present-day situation, these guarantees are offered by the world (nuclear) superpowers, standard-bearers of the great ideological positions. Willingly or unwillingly, directly or indirectly, the superpowers are involved in local wars, which appear as phases or moments of the multiple third world war that I mentioned above.

The situation appears all the more serious if we consider that local conflicts do not escape the characteristics of the contemporary war phenomenon resulting from the deprofessionalization of warfare and the adoption of the revolutionary ideology of the *armed nation*.[24] In short, the war becomes: (*a*) *industrialized* and therefore general—so that the distinction between military and civilian disappears and every activity becomes a lawful military objective; (*b*) *popular*—it therefore implies a mobilization of the minds through a Manichean propaganda that impresses upon it the character of a dramatic alternative in which the "whole" of the social body is at stake; (*c*) *ideological*, even if only in appearance—

23. "Überwindung der Metaphysik," [Overcoming of metaphysics], in *Vorträge und Aufsätze*, pp. 83–84.

24. By this I do not wish to appear nostalgic for the professionalization of war. Such professionalization reached the peak of its truth (and its paradox) with the mercenary armies, which were very concerned with sparing their men, in view of their lucrative professionalism, and cared little about respecting unarmed civilians; it is enough to refer to the celebrated judgment by Machiavelli (*The Prince*, chap. 12). I would like only to indicate that the deprofessionalization of war did not bring about the peace naïvely hoped for. On the contrary! This means that the true problem is ontological-moral, and not sociological-ideological.

because mobilization and propaganda reach the highest effectiveness when conflict is presented in global ideological terms as a conflict not of interest but of opposite conceptions of the world: of ideologies.

For all the reasons indicated, today's warlike conflicts are subject, in one sense, to ideological fanaticization and, in another, to the utilization of (or indeed, to the transformation into) guerrilla wars with their terrorist corollaries. We will see shortly the consequences of this transformation. For the time being I point out that war violence: (*a*) has not diminished, as was hoped in the nineteenth century, but has spread widely, even if it has remained below the peak of total thermonuclear violence; (*b*) penetrates, when war breaks out, every level of society.

THE RECRUDESCENCE OF REVOLUTIONARY VIOLENCE

First of all, we must acknowledge a significant reversal of the criterion of perception and evaluation of revolution. In the nineteenth century, as we have seen, revolution was considered and legitimized (by its supporters) as an organized, disciplined, and passionless conflict patterned on war: this is a point on which, following in the footsteps of Marx and even of Bakunin, Sorel insisted more strongly than anyone else.[25] Today the opposite is true. While war is always more generally deprecated and condemned (even if waged as frequently or more so than ever), revolution is increasingly appreciated, though sometimes only in words. It is not evaluated according to the parameters used to distinguish just from unjust wars: revolution is always just. So, by reversing Sorel's judgment, one may say that today war is legitimized only to the extent that it is revolutionary, that its ideal as well as its practical model is the revolution (as we shall see shortly).

Since I am limiting myself for the time being to pointing out a

25. Cf. Sorel, *Réflexions sur la violence*, 5th ed. (Paris, 1921), pp. 161, 168ff, 246ff. See Bakunin, *Libertà e rivoluzione* [Liberty and revolution] (Naples, 1968), pp. 192–94.

tendency, I shall not dwell on the reasons for this reversal. Rather, it matters more to investigate the stages of the recrudescence of revolutionary violence.

The first stage is represented by the October Revolution, which marks the end of the deterministic-evolutionistic conception of revolution and, therefore, of its tendentially peaceful character. Revolution becomes again fundamentally an act of the will, a "praxis which overturns," and no more a "praxis which overturns itself" through an anonymous historical necessity. Not only is this willful praxis decisively and materially violent but it is no longer satisfied with a "general strike." This, in the interpretation of the major theorist Sorel, is (almost) a peaceful material means, whose violence is predominantly symbolic, whose revolutionary efficacy derives from the very structure of the "bourgeois" industrial-productive system. In fact, the voluntaristic action of general strike, by blocking the entire economic structure, shows where the power of the industrial society actually lies and, therefore, produces the result of *necessarily* transferring the power to the proper holder. Also, this singular mixture of voluntarism and determinism vanishes, as the evolutionism of the social-democratic revisionists did with the Leninist Revolution. This finds expression in the armed conquest of power becoming the genuinely essential moment of revolution. It is only from the (pretended) political-state superstructure, that is, from the conquest of it, that the overturning of the (pretended) economic structure may emerge, and not vice-versa.[26]

The revolution, then, again becomes a willful and bloody act

26. And then the series of overthrowings continued: Marx had meant to overturn Hegel by putting the material processes of production in the place of the processes of ideas; then Lenin overturned Marx by placing material power (force) in the place of economic activity. We must remember Lenin's fierce struggle against the "economists" in order to give the working class a "political consciousness," which can come only "from outside the economic struggle." Cf. *Che fare?* [What is to be done?] in V. Lenin, *Opere scelte* (Moscow, 1949), 1: 192ff.

that does not *show* where the real power lies but imposes it in its violent struggle. It is the surgeon who performs the Caesarean section and by willful intervention brings the newborn to life; it is not the midwife who assists in a natural birth. Setting aside the metaphor, the determinism of historical materialism is suspended and it transforms itself into a myth that stimulates the revolutionary action that alone can realize it. Consequently, proletarian self-consciousness is replaced by the (active, thinking) proletarian avant-garde—the party that is the harbinger of events and the custodian of the sense of history.[27]

But the revolution that anticipates history cannot exhaust itself in the conquest of central power and in the seizing of legislative power: a decree is not enough to eradicate private property; it is necessary to have general authority over society and consequently to spread violent action. So the St. Petersburg Revolution is continued through the Red Army, in which the land-hungry peasants' violence of Budenny's "Horsemen Army" joins the cold technological violence of Trotsky's armored train.[28] The revolutionary war is implicit in a voluntaristic revolution, which can no longer be entrusted only with the "arms of criticism," but which needs the "criticism of arms"—as the young Marx already well understood[29]—to reacquire all of its charge of violence.

But this is not all. It is vital to remember the image in which

27. "The working class, with its own forces alone, is able only to elaborate a trade unionist consciousness," Lenin writes in 1904; and he hastens to add: "The political struggle of social democracy is much wider and more complex than the economic struggle of the workers against the masters and against government . . . and for these reasons, the organization of a social-democratic revolutionary party must necessarily *be distinct* from the organization of the workers for the economic struggle." (*Che fare?* in *Opera scelte*, p. 215).

28. The epic of the first is sung by Isaak Babel; the second flashes in the pages of *Doctor Zhivago* by Boris Pasternak.

29. Marx, Introduzione to "Critica della filosofia del diritto di Hegel" [Critique of Hegel's Philosophy of Right], in *Scritti politici giovanili*, ed. L. Firpo (Turin, 1950), p. 404.

the Leninist Revolution was perceived by Lenin's contemporaries—
an image that was kept tenaciously alive for decades despite the
contradiction of the facts. It appeared as the unexpected, astounding, and immediate realization of a utopian classless society without private property, self-managed from below (it is the myth of
the *soviet*, actualized in reality only during *l'espace d'un matin*) and
therefore without domination from above. The striking power of
this image on public opinion (on the one hand enthusiastic, on the
other disconcerted) will never be emphasized enough. The ideal
that reformist Marxism declared certain but put off to an ever-
fleeting future now seemed realized by the Leninist insurrection
through a merciless and clean cut into the fabric of history. It is
not without reason that old Sorel, who was a scornful adversary
of reformist and parliamentarized socialism, became enthusiastic
about Lenin. The basis of renovation then came to be the *voluntaristic and violent* revolution—and only *this* appeared henceforth
worthy of the name of revolution. With it, violence was legitimized and ennobled, not only as a realistic and indispensable
means of action but primarily as the brilliant and glorious "becoming present" of a new history. Revolution is the mode in
which history actualizes itself. This is the profound meaning of
the Trotsky-Leninist idea (otherwise very confused) of permanent
revolution.

The second stage of the renewed fortune of the idea of revolution is much more difficult to characterize because of the complexity and ambiguity of its itinerary, from Stalin's rise to absolute
power to the current conflict within the Marxist ideology between
the Soviet Union and Mao Tse-tung's China. It is a long journey
that sets in contrast all of recent history and of which only the
dominant aspect can be indicated.

The victory of Stalin over Trotsky on the one hand marks
without doubt an end to the hope for an immediate world revolution; on the other, it concentrates the revolutionary hope in the
"fatherland of socialism" raised to a propelling myth. By one of
the so many paradoxes of history, the remarkable extension of the
"socialist camp" is not due to the rekindling of revolution but to
the victory of the "Great Patriotic War"—as the conflict with

Hitler is officially called (and probably felt to be) in Russia—and to the diplomatic skill of Stalin. It seems that the Revolution is again disciplining itself, becoming integrated into the ranks, now organized and hierarchized, of the powerful Red Army and obeying the well-calculated schemes and strategic-political objectives of Soviet policy. Only at this price does the revolutionary project become effective and extend itself again: but by paying this price does not the revolutionary project end in perverting itself? The new, more certain way to socialism would in fact be that of state power.

Nevertheless, the paradox may find its explanation precisely in the myth of the "fatherland of socialism" and in a leader who embodies it: its every progress appears in itself to be an objective progress of the Revolution. But will this really resolve the paradox or will it instead deepen it under a mystifying appearance? In truth, one cannot help asking whether the *progress of revolution*, understood in that manner, does not resolve itself into *revolution as progress*, that is, as a gradual movement that is less revolutionary the more it is articulated according to the strategic-diplomatic necessity. From this perspective, in fact, revolution loses the character of an act in which means and end are fused in an unbreakable unity: the new praxis of history, which consists not so much in reaching this or that objective, but in revolutionizing per se. On the other hand, the revolutionary cause (in its objectivity) comes to be separated from the praxis-revolution: the former advances without the latter, using the traditional means of politics, through which it advances further (Stalin prevails over Trotsky).

But such a dissociation can save the idea of the Revolution only while the myth of the "fatherland of socialism" stands, in which the stateless of the bourgeois pseudo-fatherlands can recognize themselves as citizens. Only as long as that myth stands is it plausible to hold that the objective cause of revolution is to advance by the traditional nonrevolutionary means, contrary to the objective cause of a new Great Power, which is revolutionary in name only. But the myth has now vanished and so has opened the way to the third stage of the idea of revolution, in which violence again becomes necessary. The revelations of the Twentieth Congress of the Soviet Communist Party strike hard at that myth, introducing an irreparable schism between the fatherland of socialism and its leader. If he was an overpowering and narcissistic tyrant (the cult of personality), capable of diverting the Revolution from the orthodox line of Leninism, precisely as Stalin appears to have done according to Khrushchev's report, then the cause of the Revolution did not progress under him, at least not internally. Objectively, the "fatherland of socialism" was no longer untainted. But the fatal blow was dealt by the Sino-Soviet conflict, which, by duplicating the fatherland of socialism, destroyed the very idea of it. An internationalist movement can content itself temporarily with the prospect of a universal fatherland; but it cannot have two, for the division is the negation of universality. From the moment of division, in fact, both vie to appropriate the (indivisible) myth of international patriotism, and they exchange ever more atrocious accusations: bureaucratism, deviationism, despotism, imperialism. A despotic and imperialist socialism ought to be a *contradiction in terms*. But at this point one might ask: does the contradiction lie in the adjective or in the substantive?

All this may seem far removed from the question of revolutionary violence; in reality it constitutes the setting in which revolutionary violence today plays its role and finds its explanation. The end of the socialist fatherland brutally brings back its faithfuls to the condition of statelessness. The reciprocal accusations of degeneration of the socialist systems no longer permit consideration of them as realizations of utopia. The possibility of proposing them as models disappears, and where and how can one find others? The revolutionary is forced to this choice: either to give up the path of the Revolution by declaring it a failure and returning to reformism or to bring the Revolution to the fullness of its integrally praxistic meaning.

If with socialism the state flourishes rather than declines, and as a result the systems and the fatherlands with a revolutionary intent end by revealing the hard face of power and imperialism, then the *antisystem* is in order—the radical rejection of every institution, since evil lies not in the ideological orientations of the systems and institutions but in the fact that they are structures.

Once the structures are rejected (having been reduced to mere provisional consolidations of praxis), the radical rejection of any concession or gradual transition becomes imperative, even of those accepted by Trotsky when he exhorted the proletariat to assimilate the "bourgeois" culture before creating one of its own.[30] Only a total negation of the present as well as of the past and the affirmation of the new because it is new (that is, of the will of praxis insofar as "self" creating praxis)[31] appear to be in a position to reopen a terrestrial space to absolute hope. When all vegetation becomes spoiled or sterile, there is nothing to do but uproot it completely, overturning the ground with a spade that digs deeply and thus restores fertility. Disappointed with the models it realized, revolution must, therefore, *first* reduce history to a desert in order, *later*, to be able to traverse it in a new liberating "exodus" toward a new Promised Land, which is completely unknown, since it has no models nor can it have, these having either failed or been repudiated because they would somehow again be rational structures destined to transform themselves into institutional structures, thereby curbing the praxis. The new Promised Land, unknown and impossible to define—is it then only a dream, a mirage? What conceals its oneiric character is in fact the impatient necessity for crossing the desert, a desert formed in one's own mind (even before it existed in reality) by denying all of history, reducing it to violence only.

But in the desert there are no points of orientation that are not as vertical as the fixed stars, but all vertical positions are excluded from radical revolutionary immanence. Thus, the wanderings with neither anchor nor compass clearly described by one of the most acute French philosophers of our day, Jean Brun,[32] acquire

30. Cf. Trotsky, *Letteratura e rivoluzione* (Turin, 1973), p. 171ff.

31. "The consciousness that the continuum of history must be eliminated is proper for the revolutionary classes at the moment of their action," writes W. Benjamin in "Tesi di filosofia della storia," no. 15 in *Angelus Novus* (Turin, 1962), p. 80.

32. See his magisterial essay *Les vagabonds de l'Occident* (Paris, 1976) and his *La nudité humaine* (Paris, 1973).

mass dimension and endemic diffusion. As long as the insuppressible exigency of the subject not to reduce himself entirely to things, lands, fatherlands, and history but to look beyond at the boundless horizon remains inward, it bears fruits of a universal beauty and inexhaustible knowledge, which is everyone's patrimony, in which everyone can find himself in the common humanity—and recapture it. Projected outward, translated integrally into a self-regulatory praxis, that exigency gives the illusion that the genuine way to be free and sovereign is, for man, a total and ruthless iconoclasty. And this, following a rigorous as well as a foolish coherence, leads to the disintegration of the supreme icon of God, man himself. History, the *res gestae* of man, cannot be destroyed with impunity without also destroying the author.

Thus, precisely because past revolutions have not produced liberation and have failed in the realization of the essence of revolution or have betrayed it, the myth of the latter is proposed again with exasperated violence and resolves itself totally into violence. Doubtless, taken in their extreme coherence, these are scarcely applicable intellectualistic theses, because praxis and praxism can also be resolved into a phantasmagoric game of words and images, metaphors and dreams. But the fact is that in the latent modes of feeling and in the expressive modes of speaking (and even of gesturing and dressing), this radical and violent sense of revolution is widespread. It has acquired a fascination that easily surmounts the adverse reaction provoked in other times by the word "nihilism,"[33] totally equivalent to radical and violent revolution. Therefore, if those theses are inapplicable in their globality, nevertheless the diffused acquiescence or sympathy for them allows the explosion, even if ephemeral and circumscribed, of this type of revolution, particularly in industrialized countries.

But to the revolutionary spirit another less intellectualistic and

33. Dostoevsky expressed in an inimitable manner the double face of this reaction to nihilism: the stupefied horror (for Stavrogin, the nihilist of praxis) and the pity (for Ivan Karamazov, the nihilist of theory). What writer would today dare to express himself in either manner concerning the revolutionary?

more concrete way is open, that of symbiosis with war. This is encouraged by the fact, noted above, that contemporary revolutions have increased rather than diminished the power of the state, giving rise to the hybrid figure of the revolutionary state. Revolution, crushed because of the above-mentioned concrete impossibility of being genuinely internationalistic and universal, operates within national or ethnic arenas, from which it takes its thrusts, problems, and forms, developing traditional (even ancestral) and new motives that are very difficult to disentangle and assuming national-revolutionary aspects according to the anticipatory intuition by Mazzini.[34] The double value of the term "liberation," which may designate the liberation from foreign as well as domestic domination, favors the espousal of revolution and war. The most evident examples are the revolutionary movements in Latin America caused by the equation established there between "Yankee" and "capitalism." In a sometimes genuine, sometimes artificial combination, both explosive, the nationalist movements assume social-revolutionary characteristics while the revolutionary movements assume nationalist traits. The right and the left merge despite their ideological and personal ambiguities.

On the other hand, the persistence of state conflicts (and the resultant spreading of local wars) and the psychological repudiation of wars of supremacy make a war, as I have noted above, appear to be justifiable only if brought about by revolutionary aims. From the standpoint of violence, this fact has very relevant consequences. The mode of today's conflict thus comes to change. It is no longer only the "people's war," in which the entire social body takes part since the war mobilizes all activities (military as well as productive, intellectual, scientific, etc.) within their respective areas of action, but it becomes, in a method typical of revolution, the "people's guerrilla war" in which the entire population, including children, women, and old men, is directly involved in military endeavors. In the guerrilla war not only is everything

34. To whom, however, the destructive radicality of violence was foreign. Remember his polemics with Bakunin.

aimed at military purposes but everyone is a combatant, and the more effective he is the less he appears to be so.

There is doubtless something exalting in this global participation of a people put to the test of a hard struggle. But the critical spirit cannot help noting—outside the extreme case of defense against the impending threat of genocide—that guerrilla war demands and provokes the fanaticization of the soul, cancels every differentiation of means, every distinction between innocence and culpability, every sense of respect and pity. In guerrilla war, the spiral of violence develops with an increasingly stormy rhythm, destroying not only the body but also the soul. Though his observations were incidental, the very prophet who extolled power above any law, Nietzsche, clearly grasped the intrinsic corruption of guerrilla war: "How every long war which is not conducted with open violence makes people venomous, astute, wicked! How a long fear, a long watch over the enemy, a possible enemy make us *personal!*" [35] And Trotsky echoes Nietzsche: "Civil war is the most cruel of all wars. It cannot be conceived without violence exercised on other people and, considering modern technology, without the killing of old men and children . . . not to mention the telling of all the lies. War is inconceivable without lies, just as a machine is inconceivable without grease." [36]

In truth, in guerrilla war (and in terrorism, which is the most intense expression of guerrilla war), violence permeates the very heart of the individual because the conflict does not filter through the great collective organizations that are the armies, in which it is possible (though difficult) to keep a control upon judgment and feeling toward the enemy. In the mobility and latency of guerrilla war (which can emerge everywhere and from everyone) the encounter is always impending as a direct and personal threat and it arouses a constant fear-hate tension that discharges itself in the commission of violence.

35. Nietzsche, *Al di là del bene e del male*, aphorism 25, p. 32.
36. "La nostra morale e la loro" [Our morality and theirs], in L. Trotsky, *Letteratura, arte, libertà* (Milan, 1958), pp. 155–56.

Let us put two and two together. The recourse seems indeed to have swept away the laborious results of the course, its idealistic certitudes, the very method according to which it operated: the disciplining of violence by means of the law. It is not coincidental that the nineteenth century is the age of the great juridical theories and constructions, while our times seem to devalue nothing more than they do the law, reducing it to a mere political instrument or despising it as "legalism." A world that tended toward an order either discovered in history or scientifically devised and programmed is replaced by a world that prefers the creative or liberating disorder in both social and individual relations. In the events of this spreading recourse through so many avenues—factual, psychological, ideological, artistic—violence appears as the queen of the world, its ultimate hope. But what is violence? Both those who exalt it and those who fear it, while being under its obscure spell, have not bothered to indicate its features, taking them for granted. It is time now to determine these features with precision.

Chapter 3
The violent act and its phenomenology

Distinguish in order to understand

The rapidity and the invasiveness of the recourse, if they do not allow one to escape, even for a moment, the massive presence of violence, may well prevent understanding of its precise connotation and denotation, as the apocalyptical viewpoint illustrates. Reality and the profound meaning of human life seem clear and visible only in the darkness of night into which we are thrown by violence—the violence that sweeps away every sunny or serene vision of life as if it were a comforting delusion or a fantastic sublimation. But it is precisely in the face of such an all-encompassing feeling of the phenomenon—in which violence appears as the whole of life, its totality—that the reflective man (and the man of common sense as well) cannot help being in disagreement, particularly on the question of method, which precedes any intended exorcism or axiological renunciation of violence. In the completeness of violence's presence, in fact, one loses every sense and awareness of the specificity of the various phenomena: in the dark all cows look black, in Hegel's words.

Not only is the sense of life's richness thus lost, but so is the very sense of violence. If all is violence, without exception, then nothing is violence, since the possible term of comparison (in relation to which violence acquires distinct definition as a specific behavior identifiable in itself) is lacking (or, better, obliterated). Nor would it be to any avail to counter that indistinction would not be total, since violence would always have, within its own universe, different degrees of intensity like the circles, gyres, and pits of Dante's *Inferno*. But Dante's hell has a point of reference *outside itself*, without which any taxonomy of sins and sinners would be impossible. And, in truth, if violence can be classified according to degree, that is, according to whether it is more or less violent, then it is more or less itself to the extent that it is more or less impermeable to anything else. Between the desolate weeping of Francesca and the blasphemies of Vanni Fucci ("Take that, God, for at Thee I aim them") [Dante, *Inferno*, XXV, 3], there is an abyss like that between the nostalgia for and the rejection of good. In the gradation of violence's intensity, the immanent presence of something other than violence is decisive, whatever its name or the reality may be. Moreover, he who uses violence does not wish to be subjected to it: the revolutionary condemns counterrevolutionary violence.

Therefore, the reflective man—whether he wants "to distinguish in order to unify," following the road to knowledge from Plato's *Phaedrus* (265d–266b) to the works of Jacques Maritain, or whether he wants to distinguish in order to calculate and construct, following the way of technical intelligence—cannot accept the verdict of a total indistinction, even when it seems to be imposed by the invasive historical presence of a phenomenon. It is necessary, then, to distinguish and in order to do so one must first proceed to a comparison.

But a comparison with what? The temptation to try the most direct way is strong: to compare violence with anything that in the most common linguistic usage and in the most immediate experience appears to be the thing furthest removed from it—charity, for instance, which in St. Paul's definition "is patient, benign, . . . is not moved by anger, does not take into account the wrong received, excuses everything, believes everything, hopes for everything, endures everything."[1] These few words are enough to show the insurmountable difference between the two phenomena. Such a comparison gives rise, then, to a precise antinomy of thesis and antithesis sharply counterposed so that it does not allow equivocal proximity or too easy syntheses. It is certainly the shortest way and not at all the wrong one; however, it risks appearing like an oversimplification precisely because of the drastic nature of the contrast that it puts before our eyes. The antinomy could be perceived as based on an a priori reciprocal negation, either intellectualistic or emotive. It would be better, then, to proceed by the slowest method in exploring the *genus proximum* and the *differentia specifica*. Besides, this seems the best way to submit the fabric of existence for examination and to ascertain if its total unity is resolved into an all-encompassing uniformity or a complicated network of diverse behaviors and opinions.

In this perspective, the comparison that must preliminarily be made is, in my opinion, between violence and force. Here we doubtlessly enter a grey area, whose aspects are still badly defined and consequently in need of clarification. Indeed, if even in serious works force is very often identified or confused with violence,[2] if certainly they have many aspects in common, the fact is that in everyday experience and in our own language (which is a significant manifestation of experience) force does not appear entirely linked to violence.

Force and violence: an extrinsic differentiation

A comparison between the two phenomena, for the purpose of distinguishing them, requires criteria capable of showing their di-

1. Cor. 1:13.
2. Cf. Alain, *Politique* (Paris, 1952), pp. 10–11, 200, 277, and passim; H. Arendt, *Sulla violenza* (Milan, 1971), p. 56. Reversing current opinions, Sorel on the one hand appreciates violence more than force; on the other, as I have already noted, he confers upon vio-

versity. In the following paragraphs I shall examine the three criteria most widely used in the literature on the subject.

THE CRITERION OF THE PHYSICAL
NATURE OR THE QUALITY OF ACTION

According to a widely held opinion, violence takes on a concrete
form through a *physical* conflict between men[3] or, as some describe it, through an intentional *physical* attack upon the *physical*
being of other men.[4] In favor of this definition is the obvious fact
that violence, in general, causes physical damage, injury, and
sometimes even death and, therefore, arouses general fear and reprobation. Its physical nature appears at first sight, then, to be a
valid criterion for distinguishing violence from force, since the
latter is not exclusively physical nor does it act exclusively on
others' physical being. Indeed, the term "force"—aside from its
metaphoric use in connection with reasoning, style, or artistic expression—can be used very fittingly to designate an action that is
neither physical nor exercised on the body but is imposed on the
mind, regardless of the meaning attributed to it. The distinction
is illustrated in this example: "force" (of the spirit) is necessary to
resist (or to incite to resistance of) (physical) "violence" from
others, such as the use of torture, for example, but only the second is violence, certainly not the first.

It is not difficult, however, to perceive the poor discriminatory
capacity of this criterion and, consequently, the very narrow limits of its use, first of all because it leaves unresolved a large number
of cases. If there is a nonviolent spiritual force, there is also a
physical force (exercised on the body) that cannot in any way be
construed as violence. In order to rescue a person from being run

---

lence (typical of the revolution) the usual attributes belonging to
force: discipline, absence of hate, etc. *Réflexions*, pp. 257, 161.

3. Cf. M. Stoppino, "Gli usi politici della violenza," *Il Politico*,
1973: 449–53, and the literature cited in it.

4. See comments of N. Bobbio reported in "Roundtable on violence," in *Civiltà delle macchine* [Machine civilization], nos. 3 and 4
(1971): 27.

over by a train, physical action (force) is necessary and it may cause pain and physical damage; but no one would dream of characterizing it as violence. This simple example will suffice to render futile all reasoning that equates force with violence. In this hazy area, the single criterion of "physicality" is of no avail; it leaves the problem unresolved.

Second, to confine violence to the domain of physicality is completely arbitrary and contrary to reality, because there can be either nonphysical actions that are physically harmful to others—such as if someone were induced through tricky arguments or psychical stimuli to contract a physical illness—or physical actions that are harmful to the spirit, as would be the case if someone were materially prevented from writing (thoughts, letters) or speaking to others. These are actions that, not without reason, are commonly thought to constitute violence. Finally, the denial that there can be violence against the mind of another through psychological means is without foundation: think of the "affective contagion" described by Max Scheler or of the crime of plagiarism.[5] It is true that such an action is different from physical violence, but to exclude it for this reason from the domain of violence is begging the question. In short, if there is a difference between violence and force, the parameter of physicality is unable to put it in clear evidence: the difference, therefore, must be established by other means.

The institutional criterion or the qualification of the agent

According to a commonly held opinion that is also accepted on a scientific level,[6] violence is the action of the assassin but not that of the hangman, of kidnapping but not of arrest and detention.

5. On this see G. M. Flick, *La tutela della personalità nel delitto di plagio* [The protection of personality in the crime of plagiarism] (Milan, 1972).

6. Cf. H. Kelsen, *La dottrina pura del diritto* (Turin, 1966), 2:10–11, and N. Bobbio in "Roundtable on Violence" in *Civiltà delle macchine*, p. 28.

On the basis of this opinion, one can develop the following distinctions: there is force when the afflicting action is attributable, directly or indirectly, to an institution and to its legally constituted authorities; but there is violence when the afflicting action is *not* attributable to an institution, but to a nonauthorized individual. The reference to the institution (and to the qualification it confers upon the agent) constitutes therefore the differentiating criterion of afflictive actions. It is well to observe that the institutional criterion does not concern only the state. Consider the typical case of a band of thieves:[7] while its external activity constitutes violence, internally the leader's control of his followers is qualified as force, because within that circuit he is the institutional, recognized authority. Force, in short, would belong to the sphere of the "public," while violence would belong to the sphere of the "private."

But this criterion is not altogether satisfactory either. First of all, it is susceptible to being turned upside down. For the anarchist, the libertarian, and the radical individualist, the very actions of institutions are violence, not only because they inflict punishments and penalties but also because they establish directives and hierarchies. The action of the individual resisting or opposing the institution is considered, at worst, to be *counter-violence* or perhaps the expression of force (of mind, of character). But, aside from this extreme thesis—according to which every institutional form of power constitutes violence[8] and also implies some use of it—it is difficult to avoid the impression that certain regimes are violent by their very institutional structure. Such, for instance, is the despotic regime, which, not by chance, rests on fear, as Montesquieu made clear.[9] In the same way, today's scholars, such as Hannah Arendt, Zbigniew Brzezinski, Carl Friedrich, and Franz Neumann, have identified precisely in violence and terror the fundamental characteristic of the totalitarian system.[10] It is

7. Cf. St. Augustine, *De civitate Dei*, 4: 4.

8. For an effective criticism of this thesis see H. Arendt, *Sulla violenza*, p. 45ff.

9. Montesquieu, *Esprit des lois*, 3:8–10.

10. Cf. on this point the ample exposition by D. Fisichella, *Analisi del totalitarismo* (Messina-Florence, 1976). In a felicitous formula,

evident that in these cases the institutional criterion cannot exclude the violence of the act.

But the inadequacy of the criterion under consideration appears in its full light if one examines the case of so-called "self-defense." Here two private individuals are facing each other, one of whom commits violence while the other responds with acts that no one would dream of defining as violence. Now, no ordinary observer would say this difference stems from the fact that the acts of the latter individual are "authorized" by an article of the code! His common sense shows him clearly that the difference is of quite another nature: it is related to the different character of the two actions, to the structure of their relationship. But I will return to this later.

To sum up, the institutional criterion appears much too formal and too extrinsic not to be disproved by reality.

THE CRITERION OF REFERENCE TO VALUES

The insufficiency of the criteria we have just examined seems to be remedied by this third criterion, which clarifies the limits and the true meaning of the former, critically subordinating them to itself. Violence can be physical or mental, noninstitutional (private) or institutional (public), as I have pointed out above. What permits us to define it is the lack of a conscious reference to a value. A physical act is violent not when it is *physical* but when (and if) it is committed because of things like greed, selfishness, thirst for power, or rage; that is, when its cause is unworthy and unidentified with value. If such is the cause, the spiritual act, too, will be violent; and the same can be said of a public act and of institutional actions in general.

Conversely, force can be spiritual or physical, public or private, since what permits the distinction between force and violence is the reference to a value, whether codified or not.[11] There-

---

Fisichella defines totalitarianism as "institutionalization of disorder."

11. For Bobbio, force is justified: *Civiltà delle macchine*, nos. 3 and 4 (1971): 28.

fore, the reason that the physical act by which one defends one's own life or the life of others, or by which one captures and punishes a criminal, is not characterized as violence because such acts are motivated by and directed toward values like life, liberty, and justice, and carried out in their names.

This also explains the reason that reference is made to the other two criteria and to the basic truth underlying them. When the behavior that spills over into the spiritual or institutional or juridical domains is declared to be violence, it is not because these domains have *in themselves* any discriminatory capacity but because, by a generic and more or less conscious judgment, they are assumed implicitly to point to (or at least show a predisposition for) certain values. This is, therefore, the fundamental criterion. In this respect the following assertion by Walter Benjamin seems to be paradigmatic: "An acting cause becomes violence, in the pregnant sense of the word, only when it affects *moral* relations. The sphere of these relations is defined by the concepts of *law* and *justice*."[12] In this perspective, the criterion of reference to value (justice) establishes a means-to-an-end relationship: if the end is a value, the means will be qualified as force; if the end is not a value, the means will be qualified as violence.

Nevertheless, even this criterion does not appear to be adequate, primarily for reasons related to the very question of value, two of which are taken into consideration here. First, if we conceive of equality among a plurality of values, then it is impossible to arrive at the univocal identification of the acts (or behaviors) of violence. In fact, that which is violence in relation to a given value such as liberty, for example, may be seen as force in relation to another value such as equality, and conversely. In order to get out of equivocal situations, one must admit that the values are organized in hierarchical order. But that this is still not enough is revealed by the second problem. If we hold to a subjectivistic and relativistic conception of values (considered singly or according to a hierarchical order), it is still impossible to establish univocally and adequately what is or is not violence. In fact, an individual or

12. Cf. *Angelus novus* (Turin, 1962) p. 5 (italics mine—*SC*).

collective act considered to be legitimate, that is, nonviolent, when referred to a set of values (like liberty, equality, justice) may appear to be illegitimate, that is violent, when referred to a *different* conception of the same values and their hierarchy.

In order to get out of this impasse, it is not sufficient to indicate the necessity for referring to *recognized* values in themselves and their hierarchy, because in so doing one falls back to the institutional criterion whose inadequacy has been pointed out. In fact, the values that are *recognized* are somehow those institutionalized, either in a juridical-formal or historical-sociological manner. Moreover, the recognition is always partial or limited and transient. In short, the sociological criterion can be adequate only if we refer to *universally* recognizable values, independent of their factual institutionalization, founded ontologically in themselves and their hierarchy. Only thus can one avoid the chaotic plurality, the subjectivism and relativism of values, and the (theoretical and practical) contrasts deriving from them. But the thesis that there is an ontological foundation of values is not very popular today.

In addition, the reference to values, even when they are ontologically founded, is not sufficient to eliminate doubts about the violence of an act. It is certainly easy to distinguish a kidnapping for the purpose of extortion from the capture of an adversary as a hostage for a just cause: on the basis of the axiological criterion, there is violence in the first instance, force in the second. But the axiological criterion is no longer valid if the hostage, though captured in the name of an objectively just cause, is a neutral or a two-month-old child. One could, it is true, maintain that neutrality in regard to a just cause means no less than siding with injustice, thus ending the neutrality; and that objectively even a child belongs to the "enemy" camp. But in both cases one would have to unreasonably extend the notion of responsibility, making it contrary to general opinion, which views such kidnappings as typical manifestations of violence.[13]

13. It is for this reason that "total" war and revolution appear as violence: because they blindly hurt everyone—adversaries, neutrals,

The fact is that in order to defend or propose a value, one may proceed in different ways. There is a profound difference between petitioning and invading Parliament, even when both actions are motivated by the same value. Benjamin himself recognizes that despite the criterion of reference to values there is still "the problem as to whether violence is moral in general as a principle and also as a means to just ends. But to resolve this problem a more pertinent criterion is necessary, a distinction in the very sphere of the means, without concern for the ends to which they are employed."[14]

Even if Benjamin draws absurd conclusions, as I will show later, his observation is important from the methodological viewpoint. The criterion of reference to values, as it is generally understood, makes the act or behavior something neutral or *wertfrei* [free of value], reduces it to pure means, qualified only in relation to end, that is, in relation to something *external* to it and *heterogeneous* with it. One can say the same of the other two criteria. In the three hypotheses, the distinction between the act of violence and the act of force is made sometimes on the basis of the area in which it takes place (physicalness), sometimes on the basis of its efficient cause (the institution), and sometimes on the basis of its final cause (the value): but in itself the act remains materially the same, and this leads to confusion and ambiguities. So it is precisely the previously noted insufficiency of the three criteria, and above all of the third, which encompasses the other two, that induces us to seek the solution elsewhere. One wonders whether there might be a less *external* consideration of the relation between value and act, in the sense, that is, that the latter expresses a value in its very process of self-construction and not only in view of its finality. For instance, an act of justice would not be the one that aims at establishing and defending justice *with every means* but the one that, aiming at justice, structures and develops itself in a just

---

innocents—involving the whole of humanity in an obscure collective responsibility, even if in a (foolish) pretense of being carried out in the name of justice.

14. Benjamin, *Angelus Novus*, p. 5.

manner. Here the principle of congruity (structural and moral) between means and end comes into play, and it demands more than the extrinsic justification of the means in view of the end. But this argument would lead us too far afield. I will confine myself to saying that the inadequacy of *external* parameters to provide us with satisfactory criteria leads us to the opposite path: that of *internal* analysis of the act, in order to determine whether it can reveal structural differences between violence and force, on the basis of which a valid criterion of distinction can be established.

In search of a structural difference

The etymology of the term "violence" allows us to grasp in it a negative element: "violence" is related to "violate," so much so that rape is called violence by antonomasia. In French the connection is self-evident: the term for rape is "viol," which is the root of the word "viol-ence." This semantic profile makes violence appear to be a function of *despise* (dis-price: taking away the price [value] of a person, a situation, an institution, etc.) and to oppose *respect*: he who commits violence does not respect and he who respects does not commit violence. On the other hand, respect is not an easy or spontaneous attitude; besides a true philosophical conception of man, it demands both self-restraint and acceptance of the Other in the consciousness of a reciprocal relationship. In concrete existence, respect therefore requires an effort, a tension, in which the common linguistic usage emphasizes an element of force. In fact, the expression "He commands respect" is common; even more enlightening is the French formula: "il *force* le respect," or, "I command respect from everyone." These examples illustrate that respect evokes the idea of force, while despise [dis-price] evokes the idea of violence. The link appears even more interesting if one inverts the terms of the relationship: force arouses (or may arouse) respect to the point of admiration; violence, on the other hand, arouses resentment to the point of hatred and scorn. The analyses of Scheler are enlightening on this point.

The nexuses that link violence and force symmetrically to two such disparate attitudes as those implied in despise and respect seem to me to offer a very valid indication of the structural diversity of the former. If force can arouse respect—the respect that never manifests itself in connection with violence (that, instead, arouses fear or rebellion)—then the indication is that the difference is to be found precisely in the modes of being (of developing) of those behaviors. At the root, therefore, the difference concerns the structure of action. Let us try, then, to characterize that difference.

A useful starting point is offered to us by the completely neutral definition of force formulated by mechanics as "all that which can modify the state of rest or of rectilinear and uniform motion of a body."[15] Transferred to the level of human activity, this definition immediately requires a subdistinction, since, as is evident, one can modify a situation, a relation, or a movement in two very different ways: (*a*) through persuasion, (*b*) through imposition or constraint. But it would be superficial to believe that this is enough to distinguish the two phenomena. In the first case (from which violence is certainly excluded), it is possible, indeed, to speak of force (force of reasoning, of a personality, or of a feeling, for example), but only in a *metaphorical* sense. A reasoning is convincing not because it is "strong," but because it is truthful, rigorous, and logical, just as an example inspires imitation because it is good, courageous, and effective. In concrete reality, therefore, both force and violence fall within the domain of actions that impose and constrain, both being, that is, *activity-contra* insofar as they exercise themselves without the consent of those affected. With such actions we enter the domain of *pression* (to use Henri Bergson's term), of a relation in which there is no convergence of intentions and wills. But are we also, in both cases, within the domain of *pesanteur*, to use the symbolic term of Simone Weil,[16]

15. *Dizionario* by Lalande, s.v. "Forza."

16. Cf. *La pesanteur et la grâce* (Paris, 1948). Weil does not distinguish terminologically between force and violence but, though ambiguously, she implies it; cf. her "L'Iliade poème de la force" [The *Iliad*, poem of might].

that is, in the domain of mutual incomprehension that excludes the real human relationship? I would say no, since *pression* does not yet imply an evaluation, while *pesanteur* (in the Weilian acceptation) implies axiological negativity.

Having traced force and violence back to the *genus proximum* of the activity-contra, we are not, however, authorized to disregard the structural *differentia specifica*. In order to orient ourselves in this field, we must again take into consideration the common linguistic usage. It is customary to speak of an "explosion of violence," of "violent effort," or to say that "violence is blind," or that a person is "blinded by violence," and so on. It would not be possible to use the word "force" in the same contexts. These linguistic indications allow us to identify some structural dimensions of the act of violence that have already been popularly perceived: (*a*) *the immediacy*, since such an act reveals itself suddenly, as something that unexpectedly and boisterously frees itself ("explodes," "breaks loose"), without allowing that between will and action a distance is established in which mediation or meditation may take place; (*b*) *the discontinuity*, since the violent act does not extend itself to mediated and, therefore, "normal" activity, but is destined to exhaust itself (like every "explosion"), save that it erupts again in a different form and in a different situation; (*c*) *the disproportion to the end*, since (being immediate) the violent act, though it aims at an end, does not do so in a calculated manner (for this reason it is called "blind" or "blinded"), to the point that it often hesitates about which direction to take;[17] (*d*) *the nondurability*, since it exhausts itself more or less rapidly without ever acquiring consistent duration; (*e*) *the unexpectedness*, both of its rise and exhaustion and of its direction and result.

17. Consider, for instance, the bread revolt, described by Manzoni in *The Betrothed:* it could also be proportionate to the *motive* (the scarcity and high price of bread), but certainly not to the *end*, because bread does not become abundant or inexpensive by the pillaging of bakeries; this seems, on the other hand, to be the destiny of all *jacqueries* or peasant revolts, on which see J. Ellul, *Autopsia della rivoluzione*.

Rigorously coherent among themselves, these are, in my opinion, the principal dimensions that determine the act of violence. They are pointed out, as I have indicated, by popular perceptions with an assurance deriving from constant and direct experience with concrete reality. And it is always a perception such as this that shapes the agent (the one who habitually commits the act of violence) in a manner homogeneous to the act of violence. The violent man is generally conceived of as impulsive, inconstant, and passional, the man who obviously cannot be trusted to commit either good deeds or evil ones: in this case again lucidity and constancy are more productive. In short, he is completely different from the *strong man*, who instead inspires confidence. About what? For what? We will see shortly. In any event, we must once more note the degree of immediate and precise awareness that characterizes the difference between violence and force.

The observations hitherto made concern the violence of the *individual* act and agent. But they are also valid for the *collective* domain. The most typical collective act of violence is that committed by (or that which expresses) the most typical collective agent: the crowd. This extremely labile form of aggregation-integration, understood in a psychological-sociological and not numerical-quantitative sense, constitutes itself into a collective, unitary agent through what Scheler called the "affective contagion," by which the individual is integrated into the crowd and rises above his psychosomatic individual condition, and so loses his spiritual character.[18] The crowd's acts reveal the same syndrome as individual acts of violence: they too are sudden, intermittent, impermanent, disproportionate to the purpose, unpredictable, that is, violent. On the other hand, the specific affective contagion that aggregates a crowd is due to the (violent) impact of a violent emotion. It is the passional result of imposed pressure, of the domination exercised on a certain number of individuals either by an event (real or imaginary, but always capable of inspiring emotion) or by a person. Those who undergo this domina-

18. Cf. Scheler, Max. *Wesen und Formen der Sympathie* (Bern, 1973), p. 47; and in a more general way see chaps. 2 and 3 of part 1.

tion are reduced to useful manipulable objects by the one who dominates them: they suffer, therefore, a depersonalizing violence. On the other hand, the crowd thus aggregated appropriates the suffered violence and discharges it against others, who are in turn reduced to the object on which the crowd exercises its domination. Violence has its origins and triumphs within the circuit of depersonalization thus actuated.[19]

It is unnecessary to insist on this analysis, already amply developed by many others: it is enough to remember the studies by Gustave Le Bon, Sighele, Freud, Scheler, and, finally, the analysis by Sartre on the "group in fusion."[20] There are no doubts that the crowd is considered to be an agent of violence in the same sense as an individual is: it, too, is commonly said to be "blind," "blinded," "broken loose," and the like. Its homogeneity is such that the crowd can be considered to be the collective analogue of the violent man. The expression "a strong crowd" would be otherwise incongruous. And, moreover, everyone is aware of the difference between a strong nation and a violent nation. The hypothesis that violence does not in itself exhaust the category of *activity-contra* but that it represents a subspecies well distinguished from that of force is supported by the testimony (reported here) of popular perception. It is a matter now of passing from the notation of the phenomenological data to a deeper interpretative analysis that clarifies the data's meaning.

Measure, dialogue, coexistence

What I have so far pointed out about the act of violence (individual and collective) and the violent agent (individual and collective) evidently places them within the domain of passionality. In fact, it is passionality that impresses upon violence and the violent agent its typical, distinctive *tone* and mode of being, which is characterized by immediacy, discontinuity, and unexpectedness.

19. "The crowd . . . is the determination of animality," wrote Kierkegaard, *Diario* n. 2853 (XI¹ A 81, ed. Fabro [Brescia, 1963]).
20. Sartre, *Critique de la raison dialectique* (Paris, 1960), p. 391ff.

Here again everyday language allows us to note the difference between violence and force: while we speak of (moral) force that resists passion, we cannot say the same for violence.[21] This not only does not oppose passion but is the (possible) manifestation and effect of it. Moreover, the most frequent source of violence is precisely an experienced (suffered) passion itself. Such a passion is autonomous, outside the control of reason or other feelings; that is, it is *unruly*, not subject to any restraint. Violence is thus referred to passionality in two ways: in the way that it is produced and in the way that it reproduces its mode of being. Wherever there is violence, there is passion, even if the contrary is not always true.

Within the area of passionality, the unitary and fundamental structural character of violence, already revealed by its various phenomenological aspects (the absence of measure and the unruliness) acquires a clear relevance. What, in fact, is the element common to immediacy, discontinuity, nondurability, and unforeseeability if not indeed the absence of measure? And, on the other hand, the passion experienced in itself, in its autonomy, does not allow a limit imposed from without and is, therefore, left to its instinctiveness. But, on the opposite side, measure appears to be the typical characteristic of force, which exercises itself according to measurable times and rhythms and becomes itself, indeed, a criterion for measurement.

It appears, then, possible to distinguish within the genus *activity-contra*, force (as regularity) and violence (as unruliness). From this perspective, the *differentia specifica* is constituted by the different internal structures and is not deduced from disputable external criteria or parameters.

The recapturing of the unitary constructive structure of violence—the unruliness or absence of orderly measure—under its multifaceted external image allows us to grasp the existential meaning of a violent phenomenon. I have mentioned above in

21. It is true that we talk also of "force of passion" (perhaps to emphasize, more than anything else, *duration*), but the fact is that while force can be opposed to passion, violence cannot.

speaking of the crowd (but the observation is also valid for the individual) the depersonalizing circle in which one finds those who commit violence as well as those who suffer it. This is the first aspect to be considered, since it is the point of departure for reflection rather than the conclusion of it. In fact, within the domain of violence, depersonalization appears as *dispossession of one's self.* He who becomes the object of violence is reified; he is no longer a human individual for the agent and can even lose his self-consciousness, reducing himself, as Weil noted with penetrating acuity, to a "bare and vegetative egoism, an egoism without self."[22] But, conversely, he who takes possession of another by violence yields to it and by submitting to it dispossesses himself of his very self; he yields to the animality of which Kierkegaard speaks and he falls from his own spirituality, as Scheler says.[23] As we can see, the circle of dispossession is a precise repetition of the depersonalization that it accentuates. In this circuit the reciprocal recognition of the quality characterizing the person is annulled, "disfigured" by violence, and we can no longer recognize one another. In other terms, the common measure that equals every human being is lost or canceled.

What is the existential meaning of this process? First, we must point out that the possibility of personal communication may become lost, since it is achieved only when we have or find points in common, which constitute the criteria (the measure) of communication itself. Without these criteria, communication remains unilateral and inane, for it does not overcome the isolation nor does it arrive at any degree of intercommunication and understanding. There is, in fact, an abyss separating chit-chat from dialogue: the chatterbox speaks only to himself; the Other has for him the function of a supporting object for his narcissism, which excludes a common ground for reciprocal communication. On the contrary, dialogue, the complete and authentic form of communication (not verbal alone but practical and behavioral as well),

22. Weil, *La pesanteur et la grâce* (Paris, 1962), collection 10–18, pp. 35–36.
23. See notes 17 and 18 above.

necessarily requires a common measure. And it is this very measure that is lost in violence, which, being unruliness, denies at the root the dialogical nature of existence, and so constitutes the most explicit and radical breakdown in communication. It cannot even be said to be a unilateral communication, since it does not communicate anything: it only imposes. Unfortunately, it is not as harmless as a chat!

And this is not enough: further and deeper study of the question is possible. The cessation of the reciprocal recognition, the breaking down of dialogue, the negation of a common measure are all precise indications that we have lost the consciousness of the ontological relationship and of coexistence for which the being of man (his nature or his "being here," as Heidegger says) is a "being-with-the-other." Through the consciousness that this relationship constitutes the foundation (and the sphere) of existence, the individual understands his own true individuality, such as the "I-with-the-other" (not his fantastic, atomistic individuality), and so overcomes his latent and deadly narcissistic temptation. The individual is, then, in a position to experience coexistence as cohabitation: a solidary intertwining of human lives, each of which "has care" (the *Fürsorge* of Heidegger) of the Other. So violence brutally breaks this intertwining, refuses the dimension of otherness, and thus dissolves coexistence into material dominance.

The nonreliability of the violent man both in good and evil is thus clarified. Violence, in which he usually indulges, prevents him from dialogue and conscious coexistence, keeping him enclosed within himself. Therefore, he cannot be relied on to establish a human relationship, even if only of a mental nature. The strong man arouses confidence, on the other hand, precisely because he expresses measure, which is the condition of dialogue and cohabitation.

In conclusion, violence, considered in its structure, reveals its unmistakable, specific character and its existential meaning. It can, therefore, be defined thus: activity-contra, unruly, nondialogical, and noncoexistential. Note that it can be designated only through negations: the customary evaluative judgment of condemnation that marks it has its foundation in this structural negativity. We are therefore totally in the domain of Weilian *pesanteur:* mutual incomprehension, refusal to concern oneself with the Other, arbitrary and absolute imposition.

Chapter 4
From measure to law

What measure?

In the previous chapter it was noted that the most appropriate criterion for interpreting the manifestation of violence and, therefore, for defining it is the absence of measure, resulting in unruliness and excessiveness. This does not mean that violence is characterized by an absence of structure, since immediacy, unforeseeability, and discontinuity are found with significant regularity in individual and collective violence throughout the times and they therefore constitute its typical phenomenological structures. Rather than the absence of structures, one could speak (and this is a contradiction only in appearance) of the structure of an absence: the absence precisely of measure and regularity that characterizes impulsive acts. And consequently: where there is no measure, the act of pure violence emerges.

If, however, we stop here, we risk reducing violence to its macroscopic manifestations, which are, all things considered, less frequent. The individual who ignores or oversteps *every* limit is probably an exception; likewise, confining collective violence to the action of the crowd—although it allows us to grasp perhaps the most typical manifestation of it—means excessively limiting its presence in social life. What do I mean? I mean that the parameter of measure is doubtless essential but still too generic to permit us to draw up a precise map of violence, since its manifestations are much more complex than the ones so far examined, though they are typically symptomatic.

It becomes, therefore, indispensable to reflect briefly on the very notion of measure in order to specify it and make evident its multiple meaning. There are, in fact, many ways of measuring. I do not intend here to refer to the fact that in the field of measurement there are diverse *units* of measure both for material things (the meter or the yard, the hectare or the acre) as well as for human behaviors and facts. Besides everything else, it would be very difficult to identify, for instance, which is the unit of measure for beauty or goodness. Here I am interested, instead, in showing the different modalities through which measure manifests itself in human behavior. I see three, and an example will suffice to identify them clearly.

Let us take the case of a city policeman directing traffic. He may act *with measure*, that is, with regular and precise gestures that allow him to avoid an excessive waste of energy and that are perfectly clear to drivers and pedestrians. He may act *in accordance with measure*, that is, by applying faithfully the rules and regulations given to him. He may act *for the purpose of measure*, that is, for the purpose of establishing order in traffic. Usually these three modes are integrated: a scrupulous and zealous city policeman usually acts in these three modes at the same time. But the modes in themselves remain different, so much so that they are separable. In some of the many traffic jams in which our cities delight, the aforementioned city policeman may in fact regulate the traffic with hurried and unnecessarily tiring gestures, according to his own impulse. He acts, that is, to maintain regularity in traffic, but he does so without measure and without following the regulations prescribed to him. I am not going to dwell on the other possible combinations of the three modes, and from this example I move on to the general statement. I distinguish (a) the *internal* measure of the act, according to which one acts *with* measure (the self-measured act); (*b*) the *external* measure of the act, according to which one acts in a measured manner (measured act); (*c*) the *aim* of measure, which the act seeks to achieve (the measure-aiming act). Every one of these modes of measure expresses a homogeneous order for each of them (internal, external, purposive), which characterizes and structures the act as an *orderly one* according to that type of order.

Three specific observations are appropriate in this regard.

(1) Both the internal and the external measure are designated, in the present context, with reference to the act and not to the agent. Consequently, the first is not to be confused here with the *internal* measure dictated to the agent by his own moral conscience; nor is the *second* to be exclusively identified with the so-called heteronomous norms (in particular, the juridico-positive). The first is only the calculated organization of the act, its harmony, one could say; the second is the principle from which the act is authorized to rise and the accepted objective model to which it has to conform: it can be a juridical or a moral norm, a common tradition, or a personal lifestyle; it can be the principle drawn from the structure of a given relationship (the so-called "nature of the thing").

(2) The purposive measure is not to be identified with the *aim* of an action; it is something more complex. The aim of an action may be a value (like liberty or justice) or a generic ideal (like socialism or the garden-city). The purposive measure to which I allude refers, instead, to a precise project of organization that one intends to introduce or to an order that one intends to maintain (*a given type* of socialist society or garden-city), which confer upon the act the meaning of order. Therefore, the purposive measure is that which has an effective ordering capacity.

(3) For the determination of the *structure* of the acts, the diverse *quality* of the criteria of measurement has as yet no relevance. An act is (by virtue of its structure) self-measuring, measured, or measuring whatever the criterion of measurement: justice, usefulness, or beauty. From the structural point of view, only

the presence of any one of the criteria (according to the modes indicated above) is decisive.

A map of violence

If we now evaluate the category of activity-contra according to the triple mode of being of measure, we can throw some light on its diverse specifications and so arrive at a sufficiently precise delineation of its variegated map and not only that of pure violence. Acts-contra are, in fact, distributed between two opposite poles: the one in which measure is present in its three modalities and the one in which measure is totally absent. In the first case there is no violence. We have, it is true, an act-contra, but one in which measure displays all of its ordering capabilities by regulating it in its internal rhythms, in its rise, and in its results, so that everything in it may be foreseen and foreseeable to the utmost. So the interhuman relation is not interrupted by that act, since the act can be identified in all of its development and it therefore constitutes, one might well say, a univocal communication that leaves open the possibility of dialogue. In this case, we are faced by the kind of force described in the preceding chapter. In the second case, on the contrary, violence manifests itself in a pure state, as an original impulse. The act-contra, unruly in all of its aspects, implies only refusal and rupture; it does not aim at nor does it bring about any relation other than the unilateral one of struggling and overpowering comprised in the radical alternative of success or failure.

Between these two extreme points, how are the other types of acts-contra distributed? The immediate temptation is to establish a diagram of the quantitative-proportional type—a diagram in which violence diminishes (and force increases) in the same proportion that measure gradually introduces into the act its own modalities. However, things are not so simple: violence and force are human attitudes whose interpretation requires the Pascalian *esprit de finesse* more than the *esprit de géométrie*. If in the act *only one* of the modes of measure (and it does not matter which) is introduced, violence in itself certainly cannot grow—since one cannot go beyond violence in its pure state; but it does not diminish either. On the contrary, it acquires a higher power and becomes more dangerous and dreadful in its effects, because, in certain respects, it is calculated and justified. Let us see.

Let us consider a first case: that of a premeditated murder by a band of robbers. They do not act on the basis of an external rule and, though they have a purpose, they have no ordered plan; however, the more they conform their action to an internal measure the more effectively they carry out their violence. The criminal design, well calculated in its stages of actualization, makes some aspects of violence (its immediacy, inconstancy, disproportion) disappear, but all to the advantage of its efficacy. The second case may be that of an individual carried away by the fury of vengeance, by a lynching, or by commotion in the name of justice. Here only the *purposive measure* is present, which makes all appear permitted and abolishes the very boundaries of violence, since the end seems to justify the means. And the more the end is valued, the easier the recourse to violence becomes: it is like "cutting a head of cabbage or drinking a draught of water," as one can repeat with Hegel.[1] The third case, in which the *external measure* is present, is perhaps less easily hypothesized; an example is offered by the policeman who, while formally respecting the law, nevertheless sadistically harasses the prisoner. Spinoza formulated in principle this third case: the law of nature confers upon everyone, man or animal, *tantum juris quantum potentiae* (as much right as power), that is, the natural right to act according to one's own power, though stimulated by passions.[2] Thus the supreme measuring rule would authorize the utmost excess in human relations: the contradiction is evident. Spinoza's law of nature, in reality, is nothing more than the justification of power in its pure state, outside the law—and this is violence, acceptable only if it appears to all as a destiny without remedy, as it does to Spinoza.

To synthesize: when measure is present in only one of the two

1. *Fenomenologia dello spirito* (Florence, 1970) 2:130.
2. *Tractatus Politicus* [Political works] (Oxford: Clarendon Press, 1958), 2:3–5.

modalities, violence does not decrease at all. On the contrary, it either becomes craftier and more effective or it spreads, being justified either in its origin or in its end. Does it begin then to decrease when the measuring rule is contemporaneously present in two of its modes? From a purely quantitative point of view it would seem so, since moderation prevails over excess. And yet even this time the question is complex and does not admit a unequivocal answer. I shall consider the three possible combinations.

First, I shall examine the combination in which *internal* measure and *external* measure are present. We have then a regular and regulated activity-contra, whose goal, however, lies outside the field of measure. The result is a truncated and senseless activity, like that of a robot, since we are not able to understand its *meaning*, the *why* of its measures. He who undergoes this activity can measure it, calculate it, and foresee it in its materiality, but its meaning will remain incomprehensible and foreign to him. From his viewpoint it will objectively appear to him as violence. On the other hand, the same agent, questioned on the why of his behavior, would not know what to answer. In such a situation dialogue is impossible; indeed, can a dialogue be established where its meaning is not graspable? It does not seem so. The examples prove it.

I can cite two instances that, though of the same type, are very different as far as the relevance resulting from their violence is concerned. The first is the quite absurd one of an agent (or of a public force) acting with regularity and according to the rules but without realizing it and, therefore, without making apparent the order-oriented goal of its acts.[3] So, obviously he is truly reduced to a robot that acts without knowing why. He certainly has no intention of violence and his acts in themselves are not violent, but because of their incomprehensibility they appear to be so and result in being so for the one who suffers them. Is a robot that acts-contra perhaps not a symbol of blind force, that is, of vio-

3. I say "without realizing" since it seems impossible that the causal external measure from which he is put into motion does not also have order as its finality.

lence? However, the supposed agent is not a robot: the possibility of convincing it of the senselessness of its acts exists; therefore, its violence is, so to speak, in equilibrium.

Violence, on the contrary, is not at all in equilibrium but is in full swing in the case of the political concentration camp—clearly a novelty of our epoch of "progress." Let us set aside moral criticism of the external rule that establishes and governs the *Lager* [concentration camp]— with the "norm" of production and the inexorable punishments for those who do not respect it—and of the inflexible internal rule to which both the custodians' and the internees' acts comply.[4] Let us not concern ourselves even with the (so frequent) cases in which a double rule is abused by the sadistic arbitrariness of the rulers of the camp. The fact is that, even in the so-called "normal" Lager, the senselessness of the concentration-camp-related activity manifests itself in full. And this is evident from the exact concordance of the testimonies by those who underwent the experience in the camps of either the leftist or the rightist dictatorships. It is the very objectivity of concentration camps that imposes itself on the ideological diversities. This is already a significant symptom of the indifference, indeed, of the impermeability of this structure to any purpose. In truth, the aims of production as well as those of reeducation are negated by the obtuse inhumanity of the living conditions. The meaning of punishment is annulled by the impunity, the privileges, and the authority accorded to common criminals over political prisoners. The Lager is like a rock that crushes all those under it. It is a separate world; it is not coincidence that it is always kept hidden, isolated from the circle of information—in the same way as are the happy countries of utopia[5]—which cannot be es-

4. In the rich literature on the Lager, *Il fedele Ruslan* (1972) by G. Vladimov is the book that perhaps better than any other shows the automatism of the concentration compartments, suitably experienced (and "narrated") by a police dog.

5. This resemblance between the world of absolute utopian perfection and the world of absolute wickedness is significant: both worlds are separate (either in the idea or in the fact) from the world

tablished as a stage in a progression toward an ulterior order since its "normality" is closed to any possibility of extension.

In reality, the true aim of the Lager is annihilation: of the peasant and the autonomistic nationalities under Stalin, of the Jews under Hitler, in short, of the opponents and therefore of the will to freedom. But annihilation is, if I am allowed the pun, the end of any ordering end; it is the order of death. Consequently, between pure violence (in which measure is totally absent), lynching (in which it is present only in one mode), and the Lager, the choice is not at all a joyful one. In any event, external measure and internal measure render the Lager even more crushing and, above all, more lasting. The result is a world as its own end, in which violence, through the loss of its passional discontinuity, acquires the character of a dissolving metastasis. It is not coincidence that it was compared to cancer by Solzhenitsyn, who documented its processes and spirit with the greatest breadth and penetration.

As one can see from the examples given (and I am not able to provide more), this first combination of two modalities of measure gives results that are not very reassuring and not even, in any event, univocal. Either it leaves room for an ambiguous violence (recognizable by those who suffer it and not by the agent) or it transforms itself into dreadful violence.

Let us consider now the second combination, that in which both *internal* measure and *purposive* measure are co-present. In this case the responsibility for the reduction of violence (and, if possible, for its obliteration) falls entirely on the purposive measure in relation to which the internal measure assumes only a functional character, that of self-regulatory means in view of the goal. It behooves the proposed or established order, then, to heal the conflicts brought about inevitably by an activity-contra that, not being legitimized by an external measure, cannot help but be perceived as the rupture of a peaceful relation. It seems clear to me that the notice we take of the rupture (and therefore of the violence implicit in it) could lose its traumatic character only if two

---

of real human life, because they are projections of a design to dominate it.

precise conditions occur: the absence (or the emptying) of every possible external measure and a consensus on the final order. But these are obviously two unreal conditions. Therefore, violence will be present at least until the new order is peacefully accepted, having acquired also the modality of the external measure.

Moving from the theoretical scheme to the concrete case, I hold that the clearest example of this activity-contra is represented by revolution as understood in the modern sense. It can, in fact, be defined as a self-regulating movement with a regulating finality. It demands an internal discipline (a measure)—an "organization," as Santi Romano pointed out[6]—often so extreme as to strike at the revolutionary who acts on his own and, more significant, at those who accomplish any act of violence that comes to mind. Violence is required (and admitted) within the realm of its functionality in view of the final order, which constitutes its limit. The condemnation of terrorism by Marx and Engels and (with clever *distinguo*) by Trotsky, or of extremism as "an infantile disease" by Lenin, reveal clearly (as I said previously) the tendency of revolution to follow the model of an army and of disciplined war, as Sorel underscored.[7] On the other hand, in revolution the idea of the purposive measure is present, that is, of the order to be established, and for this reason many jurists qualify it as a normative fact.[8] It lacks, though, the external measure: in point of fact, no revolution is authorized by a rule; in point of principle, the (modern) concept of revolution rejects the very idea of an already existing rule that authorizes it. The only legitimiza-

6. *Frammenti di un dizionario giuridico* [Fragments of a juridical dictionary], s.v. "Rivoluzione e diritto" [Revolution and the law] (Milan, 1947).

7. And with him Alain, see a text of 1910 (now in *Politique*, Paris, 1952, pp. 10–12) in which he recognizes, in Sorelian language, "la discipline et les vertus guerrières" of the "socialistes d'avant-garde."

8. I, too, thought so in years long past, cf. "Per un concetto giuridico di rivoluzione" [For a juridical concept of revolution], in *Scritti in onore di Luigi Sturzo* (Rome, 1953), 1:469–93, pointing out that it is, however, always *metajuridical* (or political), never juridical.

tion, in fact, is drawn from its final cause, from the radically *new* order (which therefore rejects and cancels every prior rule) that it seeks to establish and that constitutes its *raison d'être*. In this sense revolts are not *revolutions* but rather (attempts at) *restorations*, since they appeal to the ancient order that they presume is being violated. They belong, therefore, to the already examined type of activity-contra in which only the external discipline is present.

Does violence decrease in revolution? At first sight it seems so: the activity-contra, in which it reveals itself, loses in a sense the character of blindness, disproportion, and indiscrimination that designates violence in its pure state; in another sense, it acquires meaning and dignity from its regulatory end[9] because it aims at an order. However, the discussion must be carried deeper. The activity-contra in revolution arises and is admitted within the limits of its necessity and functionality in relation to the regulatory end, the new order. This constitutes without a doubt a limit to it, but it demonstrates at the same time that the internal measure (the revolutionary "discipline") is not appreciated for itself, but only for the strength of its instrumental effectiveness. Whenever such effectiveness is lacking, the very reason to respect the internal measure falls; its presence, moreover, as we have noted, does not suffice by itself to attenuate violence, being instead able to render it more effective. Therefore, the responsibility to cleanse the revolutionary action of violence falls entirely on the regulatory end. And to accomplish exactly that, all modern revolutions propose to establish a society from which every violence and domination is forever eliminated: only on these terms does the recourse to violence appear to be justifiable.

But it is precisely here that the contradiction lies. An order (the new one) in which every relation is definitively peaceful implies the reversal and the *total* cancellation of every precedent measure and every already existing order. In itself, then, the new or-

9. Alain writes about the revolutionaries: "Ce sont les fanatiques de la justice; leur dieu est respectable" (*Politique*, p. 11). But on the ambiguity of such a justice, see, V. Mathieu, *La speranza nella rivoluzione* (Milan, 1972), pp. 135–239.

der is nothing but pure negation, which assumes an appearance of reality only from its radical contraposition to whatever stands before it. And bear in mind that it not only is a question of denying institutions, customs, and historical values considered to be anachronistic and outgrown but is the very fabric of existence, the very dual structure of man's being, in which the eternal and the contingent, the absolute and the relative, cohabit and seek and demand an existential and ever-renewed synthesis. Models (or are they only formulas?) such as "the kingdom of saints" of the English Puritan revolutionaries, the "Republic of virtue" of Robespierre, the "society of equals" of Buonarroti, and the "reversal of praxis" of Marx, clearly reveal in significant secularistic crescendo that the radical opposition of the new order to the old and the necessity for eliminating the latter totally depend on the mythical and phantasmagorical character of the former. The regulatory aim, the final order, is lost in the fog of unreality and therefore the destructive praxis is the one that will really triumph in the concreteness of revolutionary activity: the result of the oneiric myth is only a total iconoclasm, that is, violence. Revolutionary "discipline" (internal measure) limits or rejects the *individual* act of violence in favor of *collective* violence and finds, therefore, its own meaning in a higher destructive power and not in a limitation of it.[10]

Revolution cannot then but fail in its objective of *total* innovation, either by bringing about a restoration[11] or by leading to a "permanent revolution": the revolution that never ends and there-

10. Trotsky's judgment in this regard is explicit: "The questions of revolutionary morality are confused with the questions of revolutionary strategy and tactics. . . . The decisive element, in our eyes, is not the subjective movement, but the objective utility. Can such a means [terrorism] lead to the end? As far as individual terrorism is concerned, theory and experience demonstrate the contrary" (*La nostra morale e la loro*) [Our morality and theirs], in L. Trotsky, *Letteratura, arte, libertà*, (Milan, 1958), p. 167.

11. A proof of this is the excessive fear of the Soviet leaders that their revolution may reverse itself either into a new "Bonapartism"

fore, being unable ever to realize its own regulatory purpose, perpetuates violence by constantly destroying its own results and its own children. The history of revolutions is a clear demonstration of this. Truly, it is not possible either to destroy *all* the past or to *integrally* realize the dream without annihilating man himself. So the "classical" model of the modern revolution leads necessarily—for theoretical reasons, besides the historical reasons indicated in chapter 2—to present-day revolutionism, which does not propose any order but seeks the myth of a sacrificial and redeeming apocalypse. Taken in its structural meaning, revolution, therefore, does not decrease violence at all: it radicalizes violence and extends it. Not coincidentally, as I have pointed out in chapter 1, is today's positive assessment of violence closely linked to the diffusion of the myth of revolution.

Let us finally consider the third combination, in which the *external* and the *purposive* measure are both present. Although this type of activity-contra is authorized by external measure and finalized by purposive measure (both aiming at establishing an order), the lack of internal measure makes it *materially* violent. But is its meaning also violent? Let us verify it on the basis of the only real case that, I think, translates this hypothesis into practice: self-defense. In self-defense the absence of internal measure in the acts of the victim of aggression is indisputable. But unrestraint is not chosen by him; rather, it is imposed upon him by the aggressor: he who defends himself does whatever he can and whatever is provoked by the violence of others.[12] His is, therefore, a counter-violence or else, to word it with Hegel's precision, "a negation of the negation." In this case, both the external measure (deriving from the very nature of that relation, be it translated or not into

---

(of which Trotsky was accused) or into a new "Thermidor" (of which Trotsky accused Stalin).

12. I do not discuss here whether one need have recourse to self-defense or not: the absolutely nonviolent will answer in the negative. But this is a problem of nonstructural but oral order for whose difficulties I refer to B. Montanari, *Obiezione di coscienza* (Milan, 1976), chap. 2.

a norm of the positive code), which authorizes the victim of activity-contra, and the purposive measure, that is, the order that he intends to reestablish, acquire all their relief and impress upon the entire action their regulatory capacity. That which the victim of aggression *wants* is order; that which is imposed upon him by necessity is violence, which remains for him accidental in the literal meaning of the word, parenthetical in relation to his habitual behavior, and therefore also to be limited materially as much as possible. This is so much so that not only the codes but also the personal conscience perceive the negative character of excessive self-defense. And what is more important is the fact that the activity-contra on the part of the victim of aggression is viewed not only by him but also by others as being different from violence and, I would say, different even from generic activity-contra. This because, thanks to the presence of external and purposive measure (above all of the former), the behavior of the victim of aggression is comprehensible and approved by others. It escapes thus the ambiguity of a subjectivistic appraisal in order to manifest itself *objectively* as counter-violence, negation of the negation.

The analysis developed in the preceding paragraph allowed us to outline a comprehensive and sufficiently precise map of the typical manifestations of the activity-contra, identified on the basis of the varying combinations of the modalities of measure. All such manifestations, moreover, were qualified as being violent without ambiguity, except in cases where violence was in a state of equilibrium (the unconsciously acting policeman) or, not being willful, was in reality a parenthetical counter-violence (self-defense). This map confirms what I had already hinted at: the gradual conformation of the act-contra to measure does not at all determine a linear and mechanical progress toward the disappearance or the decrease of violence. It, on the contrary, becomes more complex and effective when it joins with what in the abstract is its opposite: measure.

It seems paradoxical, but reality shows us that it is precisely the intervention of measure that stops or attenuates the efficacy of that passionality that not only gives rise to violence but also dialectically provokes (because of its contingent instability) its rapid end. The presence of certain degrees or combinations of measure thus prolongs violence, conferring upon it the greater stability that passionality refuses to give it. The paradox, then, can be explained: measure reaches its integral ordinating value and its antiviolent meaning when it displays all of its essence, that is, when its three modes of being, put together, mold the action into a unity. One may observe, in fact, that where the measure is not complete the outburst of violence seems to depend upon lacking modalities: the internal and external measure as in lynching, the external measure as in revolution, the purposive measure as in the Lager. Each time responsibility seems to be attributable to the absence of a different restraining power: this is a clear sign that for the leap from violence to force no particular modality is indispensable, but all of them together are needed. If they are lacking, measure (because of its incompleteness) is degraded from a structural element characterizing a given type of behavior to a mere auxiliary element of a different type of behavior; which therefore helps and potentiates that behavior.

Must we, then, review and modify the image and the definition of violence at which we had arrived in the preceding chapter? I do not think so. Violence appeared in it as an "activity-contra— disorderly, nondialogical, and noncoexistential." It is necessary only to say: "only partially disorderly." In fact, the incomplete presence of measure, if it attenuates the unruliness (without, however, eliminating it completely), does not at all diminish (on the contrary, it specifies and hardens, so to speak) the nondialogical and the noncoexistential nature of the types of violent acts described above (with the two exceptions we pointed out). If we consider the cases we have examined, it will not be difficult to see that they are constituted of *separating* acts or relationships, not susceptible of the universalization in which Kant perceived the character of moral law and that I here consider to be, in an elementary way, the expression of coexistence. A criminal design or a lynching, a revolt or a revolution, an authorized arbitrariness of power or a Lager, are by their own nature necessarily contingent and not such as to constitute models of global and general behavior; in themselves they represent the rupture of coexistence and, therefore, violence.

Whatever one may think of these conclusions and of the analysis on which they are based, it seems to me that there is one indisputable point: where measure is present in its global dimension, that is, in the structuring co-presence of its three modalities or specifications, one cannot speak of violence in the objective sense. And one cannot speak of it in the subjective sense either, for he who acts-contra but with measure, according to measure, and for the purpose of measure, could also fall into error, though certainly he does not mean to act with violence. He who puts himself into a given structure of the action accepts or receives its qualification. Therefore, the activity-contra, structured in a unitary manner, according to triple measure is not (either objectively or subjectively) violence, but force. And this, in its full adherence to measure, does not constitute, as I have noted in the preceding paragraph, a fracture of coexistence, and it keeps open the possibility of dialogue.

Law, force, violence

What remains to be done now is to identify in its concreteness the area of experience in which the activity-contra loses the character of violence to manifest itself fully as force. In my opinion, this is the area of juridical experience. Indeed, that the juridical action, of whatever type, structures itself in the modes of measure appears evident. In the juridical domain (substantial and processual, public and private, internal and international), human behavior unfolds itself with (internal) measure, according to an (external) measure, whatever the source might be, for the purpose of obtaining a measured and an orderly life of relationship. This is true not only *ex parte objecti* (of the act) but also *ex parte subjecti* (of the agent): he who intends to behave juridically acts according to the three modalities of measure. Whenever one acts in this manner one is within the law, whether formalized or spontaneous, positive or natural (think of the "natural" obligation to pay one's gambling debts) is not important. Even he who regulates his own daily life thus, even in his solitude,[13] places himself, both because of the structure of his behavior and because of his own normative intention, in the domain of the juridical, phenomenologically intended, since he acts precisely according to the modes of measure. It is understandable, consequently, that the activity-contra, when unfolding within the juridical sphere, is not violence but force.

At this point it is necessary, however, to understand the relation between law and force, of which nowadays there is much talk, though in far different senses from the one proposed here. The suspicion arises that there is no clear distinction of structure and no correct linguistic distinction between force and violence, and that the former is hastily confused with the latter. Symptomatic of this is the change of meaning of the classical expression "the power of the law." At one time, people intended by it to describe the spiritual and moral power of the law, its authority; it was in a sense completely analogous to the meaning of the expression "the power of reason." Today, on the contrary, one alludes for the most part to the material, physical force[14] of the law, that is, to its might. If yesterday, then, one could say *cedant arma togae* [may arms be submitted to magistrates], today there are those who may think "magistracy" is exclusively at the service of the weapons or even that magistracy is a weapon itself, as revolutionary jurists and judges maintain.

Let us look closely, if briefly, at current principal modes of understanding the relation of law and force and at the ambiguities underlying them. I shall consider in the first place the thesis of the *law as force*, according to which the law is integrally reduced to force. This is an ancient thesis (I mean a temptation): in very well-known presentations Plato expounded it through Callicles in

13. Cf. the felicitous observations by V. Frosini in *La struttura del diritto* (Milan, 1962), pp. 25–26.

14. As underlined by N. Bobbio (cf. "Diritto e forza" [Law and force], in *Studi per una teoria generale del diritto*, Turin, 1970, p. 126), who, as I have pointed out above (chap. 3, note 4), intentionally defines violence as *physical* force.

Gorgias and through Thrasymachus in the *Republic*, bringing into clear light the inconsistencies. This thesis persisted and reacquired vigor and wide acceptance (losing its aristocratic status and becoming popularized) with nineteenth-century anarchists and present-day revolutionaries; antilegalism is its expression, which is both superficial and well accepted in the most diverse circles. It is evident that through such acceptance force is equated with violence.

This thesis, however, conceals an incurable theoretical vice: against all evidence it denies that juridical activity has its own phenomenological essence, attributing to it, rather, the essence of another phenomenon, precisely, that of violence. On the other hand, its clumsiness reveals itself on the level of facts: the law is not only repression and therefore violence, but on the contrary, the law is also defense, the guarantee of freedom of action. Nevertheless, in order to grasp the absurdities of the total equalizing of law and force as violence, one must consider an exemplary case: private property.

Let us assume without discussion the viewpoint that private property in itself is violence; at any rate many have maintained so, from Roussseau (*Discours sur l'inégalité*) to Pierre Proudhon and Marx. The problem then to be faced is whether property has its origin in the law: if it does, violence (at least in this case) would undoubtedly originate in the law; it would be the function of the latter to transmit the malignant infection to its creature. But the answer cannot be anything but negative: suffice it to think of the child who at a very tender age, when still ignorant of any law, peremptorily asserts "mine" first by acts and then by words. In this case, to speak of conditioning on the part of parents—and, through them, on the part of society or of a culture—is absurd: it might as easily be a question of genetic or at least hormonal conditioning! It is true, instead, that education and culture can either accentuate or attenuate or eliminate this instinctive sense of possession, which is by no means the only instinct, but the one that comes across and conflicts with other instinctual impulses.

This means that property, or at least the perception of it, exists independently of the law. Rather, this subjects wild property to an (external) measure, establishing that it be this and not that: that it not be, for example, the simple material taking possession of a thing or the possession of it in a technical legal sense. It demands that one act with internal measure: the owner is not allowed to kill those who without permission work in his land or break into his house;[15] in the most remote juridical texts it is prescribed that he react in a proportionate manner or that he follow an established procedure. Finally, it confers upon property a finality of orderliness, inserting it in an orderly system, out of which it loses its own meaning: in every juridical system expropriation is possible in various forms. In short, even if ownership were in itself violence, the law keeps it from being *structurally* so by disciplining it within the complicated network of its restraining power. Does property become for this reason a form of life to be approved unconditionally? Not at all; but the question is outside the juridical field and must be discussed on the basis of parameters different from those structurally belonging to the law. It is, however, certain that property, juridically structured—and so freedom[16] and more generally action—ceases to be unlimited and wild, ceases to be, in other words, violence. Therefore, an integral reduction of the law to force-violence conflicts with the rigor of reasoning and with the reality of facts: indeed, to think of it would mean to presuppose an imaginary original condition of always benign and peaceful freedom, an innocent freedom in its absolute form, in relation to which the law (coming from where, through whom?) could not be other than a repressive and violent imposition.

I shall now consider a second thesis, much more refined than the previous one, according to which law is the *rule of force*,[17] that is, juridical norms aimed at the exercise of physical force. Here

15. A few years ago in Rome some young men, called the Birds, entered the elegant drawing rooms of libertarian intellectuals and there relieved themselves. One wonders if those intellectuals, notorious for their antilegalism, considered the law to be violence at that moment.

16. On the authentic sense of freedom, which does not at all ignore the limits, see now R. Polin, *La liberté de notre temps* (Paris, 1977).

17. It is the thesis maintained by Bobbio in *Studi per una teoria generale del diritto*.

again there is an identification of force and violence and the former is distinguished from the latter not by its structure but because of the extrinsic addition of juridical rules. By an explicit admission of its supporters, this thesis depends on the theory according to which sanction is the essential and defining element of law. This therefore is translated into punitive-constrictive activity. I will begin from this more general point.

If the presence of a punitive-constrictive phase in the juridical experience is undeniable, it must, however, be recognized that it is not the only one, nor is it the principal one. Aside from the interest in the promotional or rewarding function of the law, recently revamped,[18] it is undeniable, despite the subtle defense of this thesis, that the law inflicts punishments and exercises coercion only in a subordinate and secondary way whenever it is not obeyed. The punishment (and more generally the threat of punishment) is an internal mechanism of the law, through which it protects and guarantees itself in particular cases of deviations from its regularity. But the general aim of the law is not to punish but to translate into the concreteness of life the human exigency of order and a protected freedom of action;[19] and, as a matter of fact, it mainly regulates and organizes coexistence and does so precisely by structuring human acts and relations according to measure. For this reason—in view of the intimate, natural human need of measure and its dialogical value—it generally arouses acceptance by conviction and not only out of fear. That it, then, does not always and everywhere lead to obedience[20] is not its peculiarity but the common destiny of every ought-to-be (moral, political, behavioral, etc.) and proves only the subordinate necessity for some

18. Precisely through the work of Bobbio, particularly "La funzione promozionale del diritto" [The promotional function of the law], in *Dalla struttura alla funzione* (Milan, 1977), pp. 13–42. For a historical study of the question, see S. Armellini, *Saggi sulla premialità del diritto nell'età moderna* (Rome, 1976).

19. Cf. my "Innocenza e diritto," in *Itinerari esistenziali del diritto* (Naples, 1972), pp. 127–44.

20. As Bobbio points out in "Diritto e forza," p. 130.

sort of sanction (in the law as well as in other cases), not its pre-eminence. Whenever men should act spontaneously in a normal way, they would act according to law without need for sanctions.

But if the law is not exclusively punitive-coercive, its norms do not aim primarily at the exercise of force. And, in fact, the consensual juridical activity (from contracts to treaties) does not concern force at all, but perhaps replaces force with reason, convenience, justice, etc.: one may say that this is an exercise of practical reason. I am referring, it is clear, to those acts in which consensus is authentic, that is, neither imposed nor obtained fraudulently; in fact, the defect of the consensus takes away its juridical character: annuls it from the juridical point of view in the popular opinion even before it happens in the sphere of positive law. But even the nonconsensual (in a technical sense) juridical rules, whether concerning behavior or organization, do not of necessity aim at the exercise of force, since they confer a structure upon the profound exigency of coexisting and promoting coexistence. Moreover, every rule concerning the exercise of force necessarily presupposes rules of behavior and organization, on the basis of which it is possible to determine illicit cases in point and, therefore, the use of force. If the law should consist only of rules concerning force, those rules would not be juridical. In reality, people act juridically not, certainly, to provoke or avoid conviction by a judge[21] but because of reciprocal agreement, cooperation, and respect, as is demonstrated in every culture by the very ancient experiences of exchange, gifts, hospitality, and oath. Indeed, one can think of the law integrally translated into rules concerning force only on condition that one imagines an original state of wicked and beastly freedom, a harmful freedom in the absolute. This is a condition as fanciful as the benign one presupposed by the previous thesis, and whose unilateral angelism is replaced here by a unilateral pessimism reminiscent of Hobbesism. But man, said Pascal, is *ni ange ni bête*.

As one can see, both theses that we have examined disregard

21. As, on the contrary, the known Kelsenian formulation of the juridical norm implies: "If A (the illicit) is, B (the judge) must."

the *structural* distinction between force and violence, hastily equat-
ing them; the second thesis, it is true, makes the distinction later,
but on the basis of an extrinsic-formal criterion that encounters
the difficulties already pointed out in the preceding chapter. Furthermore, these theses do not grasp even the full existential dimension of the law, which, as the rapid critical indications we have
just given should have already pointed out, does not exhaust itself
at all within the category of activity-contra. In juridical experience, in fact, the subjects acquire and guarantee for themselves a
precise personal *status;* they obtain the certainty and coordination
of their relations, associate themselves increasing their own individual capabilities, ensure duration to their objectified will, and
acquire safety in the face of emerging unfriendliness.[22] All this is
actuated through the patterning of action according to the modes
of measure and the commitment (neither easy nor pleasant) to respect it. It follows that the law is mainly, in essence, an *activity-
pro*, aiming at an intersubjective relation and an intergroup, pa-
cific coexistence. It is a form, one would say, of the Heideggerian
"having care," in which one *has care* of oneself-with-the-other, in
the consciousness of the indissolubility of the *Mitsein*, preserved
through the coordination of actions and relations according to the
principle of the equality of *status* of the subjects and of their wills:
the diversity of *status*, the hierarchies are of a different origin,
mostly political and economical. Consequently, for the law no
one is an enemy a priori; there is only the a posteriori transgressor
and, therefore, everyone is entitled to his own and no one must be
offended. Understood in this sense, the law appears, in one respect, as the condition for human dialogue—for there is no dialogue without reciprocal respect and without rule—and, in the
other, as its consequence, since the result of dialogue is a sure
understanding.

The law, being in essence activity-pro, aims to exclude activity-contra, not only in the aggressive and uncontrolled form of
violence but also in the measured and reasonable form of force.

22. Cf. my *Prospettive di filosofia del diritto*, 2d ed., pt. 2 (Turin,
1974), and my *Itinerari esistenziali del diritto.*

But while it excludes the former in an absolute manner, because of the radical diversity of structure that makes law and violence incompatible (where one is present the other cannot be and conversely), it does not exclude the latter in the same manner, since law and force are both structured by the fullness of measure and are therefore compatible. However, juridical activity confines force (in the structural sense that I have indicated) to a subordinate and secondary position, and so circumscribes rigorously its field of expansion. In fact, the law admits force in a very delimited and specific moment of its own activity: the moment of sanction, in a strict sense, only the moment of *penal* sanction. One can, in fact, assert that the so-called civil sanction is always pre-seen and pre-willed by the parties themselves and therefore is not understood by them as activity-contra but as negation of it (that is, negation of the civil illicit). The nullity or the possibility of annulment of an act is but the consequence of its defectiveness from the juridical viewpoint. The same is true of the forced execution and the indemnity for damages.

As for the penal sanction—the true and real activity-contra in the sphere of law—it is clear that it is force and not violence. In fact, it cannot be imposed except in accordance with measure (according to penal norms), with measure (first through a trial, which is the typical action with measure, then in the application of punishment more or less proportional to the illicit act) and with the purpose of reestablishing the equilibrium of the positions. The difference between punishment—even in its crudest form: the talion (but in how many cultures and for how many centuries has it appeared as the most evident expression of justice?)—and vengeance or lynching, and, still more, assassination, as well as the difference between jail and concentration camp, lies precisely here, and it expresses a radical change of structure from that of violence to that of force. It may be that *a given* vengeance is less painful than punishment, *a given* concentration camp more tolerable than jail, but the structural difference remains and has its bearing on the development of coexistence.

One may object to this by saying that it is impossible to separate law from violence radically by the simple act of placing them in two noncommunicating domains. Are not certain laws imposed by Hitler or Stalin (the as yet unextinguished progeny of despots) such that it would be absurd to deny their violent character? Consider, for instance, the laws that subject the individual to the arbitrariness of the mighty or to that of the political police or to the "procedures" of revolutionary "justice" in which the accused has no guarantee of defense. I shall answer: they will be juridical from the standpoint of formalistic conceptions, by which any order from the authority in power that has some exterior form is law. But they are not at all juridical from the structural viewpoint. Every order that establishes arbitrariness is not a juridical norm[23] but an act of absolute power; arbitrariness is, in fact, by definition, lawless will, which imposes itself and stands by might, not by law. So true is it that a "law" that establishes the arbitrariness of those who govern is tolerated because of powerlessness and fear:[24] to the active disproportion of arbitrariness corresponds the passive disproportion of fear that, as everyone knows, is undefinable within its own boundaries. But as soon as might no longer supports it, that "law" fails: nothing in it inspires obedience. In short, law *is*, in the verity of its concept, and *exists*, in the concreteness of its phenomenological unfolding, only when it identifies itself with measure in the fullness of its triple modality. In such a case, one can reject its historical *contents*—just as today for humanitarian reasons we reject talion, judicial torture, and the like—but its structural juridical nature cannot be denied. And this, as I have shown above, admits force but excludes violence.

While accepting the preceding conclusion, one could still repeat that it is possible de facto to use the law for the purpose of power and domination and, thus, for violence, without, however,

23. Man was conscious of it even in harsh times: the precise dispositions that limited a cruel procedure such as judiciary torture are the proof. Even the latter could not be left to arbitrariness, cf. P. Fiorelli, *La tortura giudiziaria nel diritto comune* (Milan, 1953–54).

24. Montesquieu had grasped this nexus very well when he made the *principle* of fear correspond to the *nature* of despotism, cf. *Esprit des lois* 2:2 and 9.

transforming it into arbitrariness (as in the cases cited above), but by respecting the structure of measure. I do not exclude it at all, but it is not probatory. It is not by accident that one speaks of *availing oneself* of the law: by this very fact we indicate that we are not placed at the *interior* of juridical experience but at the *exterior*. In other words: the will has not chosen the law as a regulative criterion for its own action, but as a mere instrument in the service of a completely diverse regulative criterion, that of power and domination, as in the case already mentioned. However, even in this perspective the law does not completely lose its antiviolent property. Those who hold power and choose to assert it through the law do so doubtlessly because the authority proper to the law allows them no recourse to continual (and impossible) material coercion by means of weapons, and certainly not because of a desire for justice. But by this they limit themselves and their own possibility of violence and make it possible to oppose the unruliness and arbitrariness of their acts through the law they established. Therefore, use of the law for the purpose of domination is ambivalent: if in a sense it favors the power that results in a less restive obedience, in another it forces such a power to justify itself somehow in the face of the principle of measure and to limit itself, thus mitigating the power itself. In the light of the considerations we have made, the ambiguous expression "violence of the institutions," very widespread today, is also clarified. If this expression is to mean violence of *some* institutions, we fall into the above-examined cases; if, instead, it is to mean that *every* institution is in itself violent, we fall into the angelism of the original innocent freedom needing no institutions.

The structural relations between law, force, and violence should by now be clear. What associates the first two, separating them clearly from the third, is the full presence of measure. But while force is only measured activity-contra (different from violence), the law also structures primarily its own activity-pro in the modes of measure. Therefore, it not only opposes itself to violence but it goes beyond force, beyond the entire activity-contra.

Chapter 5

Why violence? I: A law without foundation

Antiformalism: a judgment by Simmel

The structural analysis conducted in the two preceding chapters is not yet exhausted. In fact, the distinction-opposition of the phenomena of violence and force that we have described, as well as the typical existential "places" where violence and force manifest themselves, offer us a solid objective basis for a better understanding of what is mainly at stake in the substitution of the present-day recourse of violence for the promising nineteenth-century antiviolent course. Moreover, the results of our analysis will help us clarify not only the *how* of violence but also the *why* and the cultural roots of its recurrence.

In chapter 2 I have shown some of the concrete objectives and realizations that allow us to speak of the antiviolent spirit and willfulness of the last century: from the rule of law to urban civilization, from the disciplining of war through the *ius belli* to the disciplining of revolution through the rationalization of its causes and its acts. Such facts and tendencies have a cultural explanation on which we must now dwell briefly.

A comprehensive look shows the nineteenth century to be marked in the Western world, as far as culture and mentality are concerned, by an extraordinary confidence in the idea of measure, whose ordering and formative capacity is expressed by sure and inviolable laws (in the broad sense of the word). At the vanguard of such a tendency is science. Proceeding at a rapid pace on the road already opened by astronomy, science now presents a world entirely measured in its physical dimensions (or soon to be measurable, it is believed). Chemistry determined the weights of the elements and their combinations, the structure and morphology of molecules; Mendel established the laws of heredity and Darwin those of evolution. Nature appeared to be liberated from the mystery of its existence (if not yet from that of its origin) thanks to precise knowledge of its measurements, the regularity of its laws, and the necessity of its events. The calculations based on Newton's law permitted us to determine the presence of unknown planets (Neptune in 1846) and stars (Sirius B in 1861): the regularity of the world makes possible the "astronomy of the invisible," while Mendeleyev's table offered sure indications of elements not yet observed.

The immense fascination with the natural sciences and their rigorous certitudes stirs analogous undertakings in the field of human activities. There are some who attempt to join the physical and the moral according to deterministic laws: either starting from science—as in the attempts that go from Gall's phrenology to Lombroso's criminology—or from philosophy, as Engels did with dialectical materialism. But setting aside these ambiguous attempts whose results have been very dubious, the most traveled road is the utilization in the human field of the scientific methodology of observation and calculation. With Malthus, demography enunciated nothing less than the "principles of population," and on their basis he calculated forecasts that he held to be accurate. For its part, economics discovered "iron" laws regarding wages and costs and exchanges. Comte elaborated on the new science of society, sociology, as a "social physics" and placed it at the top of an organic system of all the sciences. Moreover, the importance of the nineteenth-century sense of measure is shown by the extraordinary boom in laws in that century: on the normative level a very high degree of certainty and organicity was attained by codification—not coincidentally did the century begin and end with two of the greatest modern codifications, the French and the German—and with written constitutions. On the theoretical level, juridical science refined a rigorous system of concepts, while in the vibrant pages of Jhering's *Kampf für Recht* [The struggle for law] the ethical value of juridical life was exalted. Not even ethics escaped the influence of the idea of law: this was at the center of Kantian rigorism, which was the dominant lay morality of the century, but it had no less importance in Hegel's treatment of ethics.

In the ever more complex reticle of laws, the physical and human world became clear and precise, but this could not force it to a static position. Not only do physical evolution and the dynamism of activities follow regular rhythms and cadences but so also does historical time. A suddenly flourishing form of reflection, the philosophy of history, took charge of determining them. If Hegel's philosophy of history analyzed in retrospect the times and forms of the dialectical process toward freedom, Saint-Simon and Comte, taking inspiration from the expansion of science and from the first steps of industrial society, elaborate a philosophy of history as an unfailing progress according to the law of the "three states." Starting from economic laws, Marx constructs historical materialism and therefore a very different philosophy of history, but one held to be no less indisputable.

It is unnecessary to multiply the examples. If different and even opposite orientations are not lacking (the rebellious romantic hero), the general tone and the dominant mentality are in favor of the idea of rule and law. On the other hand, not even Nietzsche, the great rebel, the negator of every duty and discipline, completely escapes the fascination of the rule. Whether his theme is dance, eternal return, or the cyclicity of time, the idea of rule is always present in Nietzsche's mind, although his rule is an "arbitrary" one, which only the exceptional man, the superman, he who knows how to be "master," is capable of understanding and imposing.[1]

In a cultural climate in which the natural world appears to be comprehensible and the human world interpretable and constructible in terms of rule, regularity, and law, it is clear that one tends toward minimizing and overcoming violence that is unruliness and immoderation. Not coincidentally, at the end of that historical-cultural age, did Émile Durkheim elaborate on the concept of anomie, bringing to light (and warning about) the dissolving power that the loss of the sense of law and of the order-aimed function of the values may have on both society and the individual—suicides are for Durkheim a consequence of it. The recourse of violence marks then a precise reversal of the cultural tendency: the preference moves from rule to unruliness. Under what form did this happen?

In 1918, immediately after World War I, which marked the real separation between the nineteenth and the twentieth centuries, Georg Simmel offered us a very lucid critical interpretation of that cultural change. It is worthwhile to report its principal points. Simmel's criticism is the more probatory since his *Lebensphilosophie* [Philosophy of life]—in which life in itself is described as a perennial "becoming and dying" and consequently a constant struggle between old and new forms—was predisposing him to sympathy toward the dynamism of the rising century. However, he does not fail to notice that the situation now is radicalized beyond the limit: "Life feels *form as such* almost as something imposed upon it coercively; it wishes to shatter not this or that form but form in general and absorb it into its own immediacy, in order to put itself at the place of form and let its own plenitude flow just as it springs from its source, until every knowledge, value, and structure becomes simply the direct revelation of life itself. At present we are in the middle of this new phase of the ancient

1. Cf., for example, *Al di là del bene e del male*, aphorism 188 (Milan, 1968), pp. 85–86.

struggle, which is no longer the struggle of form, today filled with life, against the old form which has become lifeless, but the struggle of life against form in general, against the principle of form."

Simmel took the cue from the success of expressionism in art in order to indicate precisely this further character of antiformalism: "Life possesses its meaning beyond the beautiful and the ugly in its bursting out without the determination of an aim and only under the impulse of force." The rejection of form is, therefore, followed by the rejection of the values from which life could receive the directive and formative criteria of its own manifestation that are now rejected. Truly, "youth is above all concerned with the process of life; it wants only to experience the forces and the excess of forces of life." Consequently, an exasperated search for originality spreads: "The passion of bringing about one's own real life acts in this, and it seems that the certainty that it is precisely *one's own* externalization is attained only when it does not retain in itself anything existing differently and traditionally." It is not surprising, therefore, if this vitalism implies not only the negation of the products of history (institutional forms, traditions, habits) but also the negation of every element of objectivity, which is dissolved into a limitless pragmatic subjectivism. Simmel punctually grasped this ulterior moment in the most recent manifestations of pragmatism: "While original pragmatism dissolved the form of the world into life only from the subjective side, a similar phenomenon now occurred also from the objective side. Nothing was left of form as the cosmic principle external to life, as the determination of the being in its own meaning and power."[2] Aside from indicating the dubiousness of considering form as a principle *external* to life, one could not say more in such a brief discussion.

At the dawn of this century, the elements on which Simmel founded his observations were really very few—expressionism and futurism in art, pragmatism in philosophy, new ideas about

2. Cf. G. Simmel, *Il conflitto della cultura moderna*, pp. 108, 117, 120, 124.

sexual morality—and might then have seemed tenuous or of scant significance. But the successive cultural developments have amply confirmed Simmel's farsighted judgment. How can we disregard atonal music and the unrestrained and expressive figurative arts or the so-called sexual liberation? From the refusal of the very principle of form to the refusal of the past; from the resolution of aesthetic, social, and moral values into the subjective appreciation of their own vitalistic manifestations, to the reduction of objective reality to man's particular sense of life: all point to a conspicuous change from the mentality of the previous century. Simmel recalls, not coincidentally, not only the great theoretical masters Kant, Hegel, Comte, or Marx, whom the twentieth century still celebrates and officially follows, but also the "hidden kings" Schopenhauer and Nietzsche, who have been neglected and have secretly undermined the bases of the thought of the great masters (who else repudiated all four, as Nietzsche did?) and thus prepared the new cultural climate. Simmel had made a direct hit. A little over ten years after these pages of his, the decisive interpretation by Heidegger revealed Nietzsche as the key thinker of the times that brought about the present-day crisis, the one who pushed it to the extreme consequences and thus clarified its essential terms.[3]

In Simmel's judgment, therefore, the new mental and temperamental climate of the twentieth century essentially distinguished itself from the past by its theoretical and practical rejection of form in general. Rejection of form or of measure? Both. Even as concerns the specific problem of violence, I still prefer to emphasize the repudiation of the sense of measure, since this is completely homogeneous with the sense of form but has priority over it because it is more closely and directly related to the structure of action. Is it perhaps too risky to say that form is the expression of measure?[4] Therefore, rejection of the sense of measure

3. But before Simmel and Heidegger, this epochal importance of Nietzsche had been grasped, perhaps better than by anybody else, by Russian thought from Dostoevsky to Sěstov.

4. This is suggested by the great classical theses on art, from

and rejection of the sense of form, far from ignoring each other, follow each other and integrate themselves. This is confirmed by the tendencies and concrete facts—which were pointed out in chapter 2—in which today's recourse of violence finds its embodiment; from the explosion of private aggressiveness to guerrilla war, from nuclear war to permanent revolution, excessiveness and inordinateness proceed together.

Antilegalism

The civilization of the nineteenth century had relied on the law to translate into the reality of social and political life its ideal of measure for eliminating violence. That the choice was neither casual nor without foundation can be seen if one considers, on the one hand, the structural nexus between law and measure and, on the other, the high level attained in that century by juridical thought and the professional preparation of jurists. The latter, always a conspicuous part of the political class, were now prevailing over their traditional rival—the military. It is not surprising, then, that in the return to violence, law and jurists are severely criticized.

In fact, one of the most definite current manifestations of the rejection of measure (and of form in Simmel's sense) is precisely *antilegalism*. This term does not designate a true and proper, well-supported and definite theory; it is rather a generic label under which is collected a heterogeneous mass of feelings and resentments asserted in both a peremptory and an approximative manner. However, the penetration of antilegalism is quite widespread in various sectors of relational life, from social to religious. Therefore, while its theoretical value is negligible, its value as a symptom of the widespread appreciation of violence is considerable. In order to understand, it is helpful to examine the already cited judgment by Walter Benjamin, in which the nexus between antilegalism and violence is clearly brought to light. As we will re-

---

Vitruvius to Leon Battista Alberti, from the *De musica* by St. Augustine to the treatises on harmony by Tartini.

member, Benjamin accurately observed that the question of violence is defined in relation to the "concepts of law and justice." But at the same time, he had vigorously denied that the question could be resolved on the basis of the value and justice of the agent's purpose.[5] The direct relation between violence and law is therefore decisive. Benjamin immediately notes the sharp opposition on the level of existing normative regulations: this is a full confirmation of the nineteenth-century tendency to eliminate violence through the law, as I mentioned above. "It is," he writes, "the universal principle of present-day European legislation that the natural aims of a single individual *necessarily* collide with juridical aims when they are pursued with any degree of violence." Benjamin consequently deepens his conception: "The law considers violence in the hands of the individual to be a risk or a threat to the juridical organization." We are then faced with the usual thesis of the monopoly of force by the juridical organization. Benjamin, however, quickly makes clear that such a monopoly is not explained "by the intention of safeguarding the juridical *ends*, but rather by that of *safeguarding the law itself*." In short, violence is considered by the law to be a menace "not because of the ends that it pursues, but simply because it exists outside the law."[6]

The central point of the question is clearly understood: between violence and law there is an opposition of essence, which is therefore permanent, and not of ends, which could be contingent. But in what does this opposition consist? Taking his cue from the revolutionary strike and from war, Benjamin attributes the opposition to the fact that violence "is in a position to found and modify juridical relations, even though the sentiment of justice may be hurt."[7] At first sight, the phrase could be understood to mean (absolutely correctly) that the law rejects violence because *materially* violence is certainly in a position to establish an order and, therefore, new norms—but only through imposition, which

5. Cf. chap. 3, notes 12, 14, this volume.
6. Cf. *Angelus novus*, pp. 8–9 (italics mine—SC).
7. Ibid., p. 11.

offends justice. Nevertheless, Benjamin does not care at all about this "offence to justice" felt by the law: if he did, he could not avoid finding himself on the side of the law on which he should bestow the merit of defending justice. In reality, Benjamin does not base his criticism of violence on the *unjust manner* (recognized as such by himself) in which violence creates the law, but on the pure and simple *fact* that it creates a juridical order. Therefore, he views the opposition of the law (which he reduces to the positive juridical organization of the state) to violence as nothing but opposition between two diverse sources of norms: one being power, the other violence. The phrase cited above must be interpreted in this sense.

Benjamin, however, does not reduce such opposition to the conflict between the established order and the need for a new order in accordance with a widespread and superficial thesis (think of the formula of *désordre établi* by Emmanuel Mounier). Benjamin's reasoning is radical in a very different way: this opposition of law to violence is lacking theoretical foundation because for him everything in the law is *already* violence, from its origin to its methods of facing and resolving conflicts (contracts as well as punishment, parliaments as well as police), since in order to impose its own rule the law is forced to resort to violence, punishment. Here, accepted uncritically, reappears the conception of the exclusively punitive function of the law. It follows that "the only sure foundation" for a serious criticism of violence lies precisely in the fact that it creates laws. Paradoxically, the fundamental fault of violence is identified by that which discloses its contingency, its instability, and marks its end because of the laborious prevalence of regularity and sense of measure. This is, in fact, the structural meaning of the rise of a new juridical order following a destructive event. In other words, for Benjamin, criticism of violence must begin with criticism of the violence that is the law, however it may come about.

This paradox is clarified, if one could say so, through a further paradox. Explicitly taking his lead from Georges Sorel, Benjamin characterizes the revolutionary strike as a "pure means of agreement," which lacks violence and is equivalent to nothing more than "conversation."[8] Note that he is not limiting himself here to approving revolutionary strike because of the justice of its cause, but without hesitation he declares it to be a *nonviolent* means of negotiating an agreement. The paradox is evident to anyone who abides by the reality of things, but not to Benjamin, who remains faithful to the premise of his doctrine. If he considers the law in itself to be violent, it logically follows that he judges the revolutionary strike to be nonviolent, since it is *anarchical*, as he explicitly says. On the other hand, he judges the general political strike to be violent (his point of departure being Sorel again), because it "puts into being a law."[9]

His discussion reaches this conclusion: there is violence only where a law is created or preserved; there is no violence where there is no law. Benjamin supports this conclusion through a disputable but illuminating contraposition between mythical violence and divine violence. He condemns the first and exalts the second in the following terms: "If mythical violence establishes the law, divine violence nullifies it; if the former sets limits and *boundaries*, the latter destroys *limitlessly;* if mythical violence inculpates and punishes, divine violence purges and expiates; if the former is impendent, the latter is fulminant; if the former is bloody, the latter is lethal and bloodless."[10]

Now everything is clear: criticism of violence not only begins with but totally resolves itself into criticism of the law, for the law imposes rules and limits to action (even to destructive action!) and watches over it. Contrarily, criticism of violence resolves itself into self-rehabilitation, providing that it is analogous to that attributed by Benjamin to the divinity, which is *pure, immediate, unlimited, purifying*. How it can then be *lethal without bloodshed* is a mystery; but for the author the important thing is that man's violence takes on a divine and metaphysical character. This is what

8. "Cette fille expirante des aristocraties oisives et des monarchies absolues," as Barbey d'Aurevilly eulogized it with rather reactionary nostalgia in his *Diaboliques*.

9. Ibid., p. 20.

10. Ibid., p. 25 (italics mine—SC).

happens in revolution, as Benjamin explains here and in a more complete manner in his *Theses on the Philosophy of History*.

The analysis carried out in chapters 3 and 4 already constitutes a refutation of the principles asserted by Benjamin. Therefore, I am not interested in discussing the matter in detail here since it is alien to any serious phenomenological inquiry into the problem, and it ignores every structural difference between violence and force, between activity-contra and activity-pro, and consequently between violence and law. On the other hand, attracted only by the problem of action in a "changeless present," Benjamin also rejects historicism; thus, his appreciation of pure violence that is capable of "making the *continuum* of history break out"[11] is based on an a priori and unwarranted ideology to be actuated by the will, not to be proved by experience and reason. Moreover, his thesis is strictly anarchical, unchanged in its simplistic substance and renewed only through sophisticated arguments.

Why, then, have I dwelt on a detailed exposition? For two reasons. First of all, because it is a *specular* confirmation of Simmel's judgment (which is almost contemporary) on the new cultural climate. While Simmel criticizes the radical rejection of form and the exaltation of immediacy of action,[12] Benjamin wants the triumph of immediacy brought to its limits and regularity. Second, because it very clearly and completely reveals in the return of violence the conceptual network of antilegalism and its compromission.

Truly, Hegel had already identified in a magisterial way the essential target of the antijuridical tendency: "The special mark which it carries on its brow is the hatred of law. . . . The formal character of the right as a duty and a law it feels as the letter, cold and dead, as a shackle . . . because law is the reason of the thing,

11. The citation comes from "Tesi di filosofia della storia" (16 : 81) in which the "pandemonium of historicism" is denounced.

12. "Life is inseparably tied to the necessity of becoming real only in the form of its opposite, which means in one *form*. . . . Here, therefore, life wants something which it cannot absolutely attain. It wants to determine and manifest itself beyond any form, in its bare immediacy" (*Il conflitto della cultura moderna* (Rome, 1976), pp. 132–33).

and reason refuses to allow feeling to warm itself at its own private hearth."[13] Once again Benjamin's position is specular, since he approved what Hegel condemned; but while Hegel aimed at the romantic rebel and therefore at individual antilegalism, Benjamin, on the contrary, dealt with collectivistic antilegalism, antilegalism that expresses itself in class revolution, as yet unknown to Hegel. The picture is thus completed and it conforms precisely to actuality. Antilegalism is not only intolerance (very often justified) of a formalistic legalism—like that which rebounds from Shylock to Portia and conversely in the *Merchant of Venice*—or of an improper transfer of the juridical spirit into a field that is not its own. It is the repudiation of law in itself, of measure and form in the name of the sovereign arbitrariness of the subject, whether individual or collective.

At the root of this rebellion against the law is, whether realized or not, a precise metaphysical position: the conception of man as God, as unlimited power, man as a "sun unto himself," to use Marx's words.[14] As Nietzsche put it, man does not tolerate not being God;[15] therefore, it is necessary for him to deny the law because the mere presence of it attests to his not being God, not pure goodness, not omnipotence. Only "if God does not exist is everything permitted," as the Nietzschean Ivan Karamazov said, and thus the illusion of omnipotence may arise. But is it enough to deny the law in order to become God? In reality, the translation into practice of this metaphysical dream implies the dissolution of the authentic sense of law as an interpersonal mode of living the *Mitsein*, a being-together whose basic element is the respect of each individual in recognition of the necessity (and value) of interpersonal relations. The place of the law is overtaken by a will to power that denies real individuality in favor of the superman, or that burns the whole of history (of which the law expresses the

13. *Filosofia del diritto*, Preface, pp. 10–11.

14. Cf. Marx, Introduction to "Critica della filosofia del diritto di Hegel," in *Scritti politici giovanili* (Turin, 1950), p. 395.

15. Cf. Nietzsche, *Così parlò Zarathustra* II, "Sulle isole beate," p. 101.

duration) in the purifying pyre of revolution. I will return to this point later. For the time being I am concerned with probing into *why* the law may have exposed itself to such repudiation, may have been mistaken for violence, and denied its fundamental meaning of "concern" for the interpersonal relation.

A fragile law

To understand the reasons for the rapid deterioration of the nineteenth-century success with the law, one must take into account the two principal theoretical (and practical) orientations that brought about, in the Western world, the contemporary image of the "juridical." I allude (1) to the particularization of law (to its state control and then to its politicization); (2) to the reduction of law to a pure act of the will (and of a contingent will).

The first of these orientations leads to the end of the universal sense of law. Nineteenth-century historicism repudiated the idea of natural law—so called because relative to man qua man and therefore connected to ontological structures of the human condition. The specific nature of law is now its own history, which is nothing more than the manifestation of the totality of the particular history of a people in their culture and the institutional forms of their way of life. From the historical point of view, in fact, mankind is divided into the various families of its peoples, each with its own experience, language, and customs. The law, then, has no universality other than the lexical; reality, which is history, knows only the different and particular juridical orders, which were created by individual peoples or by political groups in the course of their historical development. The ideal unity of the law—of which somehow the systems of natural law are meant to be the expression—is put aside in favor of the diversity of content in the juridical organizations. From an analogous negation of natural law, utilitarian empiricism (for which the law is dependent upon the particular situation and the concrete interest that it arouses) arrives at the same result.

This theoretical orientation had a very concrete precedent in the slow but tenacious political action through which the great absolute monarchies disintegrated the institutional and ideal unity of the Western Empire. Their objective was the creation of unitary and autonomous states according to the synthesizing formula: *un roi, une foi, une loi*. The nineteenth-century creation of sovereign national states crowns this work and is culturally supported by the idea of a nation as a historical individuality. Each state has its own juridical order, completely autonomous from those of other states, and independently created. The historicist negation of the idea of natural law brings about the fall of the universal sense of law and then the elimination of the concrete "common law"— whose enforcement was extended to the area of the *Res publica christianorum*—which constituted somehow the basic unitary link between the various particular legislative systems.

The nineteenth-century juridical science, for its part, accepts fully the practical lesson of the process, forming national organizations, feeling in part the influence of the theoretical orientation both historicist (like Friedrich Savigny) and utilitarian (like John Austin). It thus demands as a dogmatic premise of its work, the "end" of every single system of regulation that is self-sufficient from the conceptual point of view as well as in its normative contents. The structural unity of the law following the universal existential reasons for its existence is thus broken.

Being fragmented and resolved into many juridical systems, produced by the diverse political communities and embodied by them, the law loses not only its universality but also its own essence.[16] It becomes the mere external normative form of the exigencies of life and of the practical objectives of particular political entities. But as a result the universality of justice disappears, too. Pascal had already noticed it with disappointed accuracy when this tendency was just beginning and was still hidden under the persistent authority of the previous universalistic conception. How is one to find a universal justice if that which is held to be true on this side of the Pyrenees is held to be false on the other side? It is thus a very strange justice whose boundaries are a river

16. Cf. G. Capograssi, *Riflessioni sull'autorità e la sua crisi* (Milan, 1977), pp. 27–28.

or that changes according to the meridians. It is Pascal who noted the interdependence of these two relativizations: we no longer have a true law; otherwise we would not take the customs of our own country as the rule for justice.[17]

Nietzsche arrived at the same conclusion but he expressed it in still more general, metaphysical, and nondescriptive terms. For him, however, the sign of the triumph of the man-master is that which for Pascal demonstrated the misery of the man who relies only on himself. Nietzsche, too, in fact, related the negation of truth in itself ("Truth is not something which exists and is to be found, discovered, but something *to be created*. . . . It stands for the will to power") to the arbitrariness of justice: "The problem of *justice*. Its first element and the most powerful is naturally the will and the force to superpower. Only he who has become master subsequently institutes *justice*, that is, submits things to his own rule."[18]

The rule in general has therefore lost its own universality, since it is not linked to man as such but to the *political* man, the member of the great historical politico-national individuality. Law and justice are brought within the domain of politics,[19] by which they are now assessed, and so cease to be the rule of its assessment.

Above these particular rules (and political entities) there is what the theorists of natural law in the seventeenth and eighteenth centuries called the "state of nature," but whose directive criterion is unruliness. It is a condition, in fact, in which power dominates unchallenged—consider in particular the theories by Hobbes and Spinoza—and, finally, war, the "ultimate reason of kings," as it was called by the old political theorists. The supreme attribute of the sovereignty of every state is the power of war, which is only subjected to the calculation of political convenience or, to use

17. Cf. Pascal, *Pensées*, ed. Brunschvicg, n. 294, 297.

18. Cf., respectively, *Der Wille zur Macht* (Kroener edition, 1964), p. 377, and *Die Unschuld des Werdens* [The innocence of becoming] (Kroener edition, 1956), 2:262.

19. On the structure of politics and its differences from the law, cf. my *Itinerari esistenziale del diritto* (Naples, 1972), chap. 3.

Hegel's language, is entrusted with the state self-consciousness of every single nation that is responsible for its own behavior and destiny only to itself.[20] The law, deprived of its universality and reduced to a national individuality, no longer offers a common rule that defines war as an illicit act; it can only attempt to discipline the war through conventions, the honoring of which is at the discretion of the warring parties. The same occurs in the case of the already particularized justice, so that the judge of war-justice is success. The only defenses against unruliness are reason, morality, and religion, but they are stripped of the precious support of juridical rule and of justice.

I shall now examine the second orientation that I have mentioned: the one that considers the law to be a mere product of the will. At its origin in the modern age, we find the political voluntarism-utilitarianism of Machiavelli and Hobbes translated into practice by absolute sovereigns whose expressed intention is sufficient to create the law, which is only determined by the interest in their power and the greatness of their states. Nineteenth-century historicism of Hegelian persuasion, with its diverse repercussions in the juridical world, seemed in truth to have stopped this voluntaristic-utilitarian tendency. By rooting in the history of the various peoples their respective juridical systems, nineteenth-century historicism made of them the traditional self-creation of the national *esprit général*, to go back to an anticipatory concept of Montesquieu. Thus the laws, though particular, appeared at least to be protected from both the arbitrariness of the sovereign's will and the abstract calculative reason of the enlightenment-oriented legislator. They appeared, rather, to draw their origin and justification from unanimous historical reason. The positivistic organicism of Comte operated in an analogous sense, that is, in an anti-voluntaristic sense of its own and in the name of the progressive self-creation of history. But this was a brief interruption: juridical voluntarism soon gained the upper hand. I will point out here three factors that, in my opinion, strongly contributed to this.

First, I recall the decisive influence of Rousseau's voluntarism

20. Cf. *Philosophy of Right*, par. 334–37.

on the democratic doctrines. In truth, democracy is in his thought a rather ambiguous combination of will and tradition. In fact, it springs from and is directed by the *volonté générale* and, nevertheless, draws strength from the continuity of the national *moeurs*, without which, according to Rousseau, a people does not exist.[21] But democratic thought that follows to a large extent takes up only the first aspect of Rousseau's theory, freeing the legislative will from its dependency on the historical element represented by the *moeurs*. The law, becoming the direct expression of the *volonté générale* (while in Rousseau the relation of one to the other is more complex), finds in it its only foundation and limit. The transfer of sovereignty from the monarch to the people does not alter at all the voluntarism of legislation; indeed, it offers a better justification of it and potentiates it, since the will of *we*, the people, appears more plausible than that of *I*, the monarch. Is it perhaps not said "*voluntas populi voluntas Dei?*"

Second, there is the emergence of industrial society, with its development in the current technological age. It has provoked an intensification and an unprecedented broadening of legislative activity to keep up with the dynamism and the increasingly complex expansion of the new society. The fabric of the laws seems to move irrevocably away from the simplicity of juridical common sense, becoming more and more artificial. The thought that it still corresponds to the "spirit of the people," to their historical individuality, and to their lasting traditions becomes ever more illusory. On the other hand, the dynamism of the technological age, with its constant innovations, demands ever more contingent norms, norms of short duration, experimental and provisional, one would say. The illusion of a juridical structure, at once voluntaristic and rational, and therefore complete and enduring even if not everlasting, thus falls, too. The codes that express this tendency, after the considerable duration of the Napoleonic code, have an ever shorter life and legislation is ever more contingent.

Third, the Hegelian type of historicism, which makes history

21. On this unresolved ambiguity, see the precise observations by P. Pasqualucci, *Rousseau e Kant* (Milan, 1976), 2:409–35.

comprehensible a posteriori, that is, at the end of events, and therefore gives value to the past, is succeeded by activistic historicism of the Marxist-revolutionary type, which looks toward the future. Man is indeed history, but he is the history that he makes and will make with his activity, the history produced by his will. The law is nothing but this will in action, oriented toward producing a brand new future and destroying, thus, the past: the revolutionary decree is its typical expression and exceptional laws its constant praxis. There is no more a will aiming at that duration that holds together the past, the present, and the future in the constancy of self-discipline and regularity. Incidentally, Giovanni Gentile experienced within himself, in a dramatic manner at the end, both versions of historicism: the traditional and the revolutionary. While he desired to be the heir and custodian of the Risorgimento's traditional right wing, his philosophy contrarily celebrates the absolute freedom of pure act, the self-positing will (autoctis) that is, one could say, the mobile motor of history. And it is not coincidence that for Gentile the only true law is the one in the act of being willed. By reversing a very ancient maxim and also the title of a well-known Italian juridical book, one could say that as a result of the three factors indicated here the law reveals itself as *inconstant will*.[22]

The reduction of law to a particular and contingent will is the result of its falling within the domain of subjectivity. By this term I do not mean to allude to the irreplaceable "site" where sensibility, knowledge, and morality live concretely: and where could they do this if not in the individuality of the subject? I mean, instead, to refer to subjectivity as a new *measure* of sensibility, knowledge, and moral evaluation: no longer the man-in-the-world, the I-with-the-other, in short, the individual-in-his-relations, but the subject in his self-centered unity, in his particular existence and will, held to be self-sufficient and self-founded. It will be individual subjectivity, as in the romantic titanism of yesterday or in the very recent orientations that today refuse the rule of a universal

22. I allude to A. Pekelis, *Il diritto come volontà costante* (Padua, 1930).

morality and of the juridical objectivity in order to posit their
own individual sensibility as the rule of morality and law. The exception thus becomes the norm. It will be the collective subjectivity of man in his *magnified form*, the *great animal*—the state, as
Plato called it, or in the case of a crisis of the latter, it will be the
subjectivity of the class, of the group that has power, or of the
ideological factions, which accentuates the particularism and
the conflictual character of the will of the collective subject. Thus
the particular becomes the measure of the universal. In any event,
one is always within the domain of the measuring subjectivity[23]
whose product is now the law.

The juridical measure, in this perspective, no longer has an
anchorage with a universal significance and comprehensibility: it
stretches and shortens, enlarges and restricts itself according to
the contingent determinations of the subject's will that posits it.
Besides, it could not be otherwise, because by refusing every idea
of a common human structure it has blocked the way to the comprehension of the ontological reasons for the existence of the law
and, therefore, to the research of an existential basis of juridical
regulations. These cannot be justified except through reasons either of a necessarily contingent utility and opportunity or of a
morality that is not only particular but also exclusive. But such an
elastic and circumscribed rule in space and time will always appear to be arbitrary, in some aspects at least; nor can it escape the
suspicion of arbitrariness by justifying it as a *historical* rule, required by history or at least at the level of history. In a history that
is entirely to be made, that is resolved into the exclusive dimension of the future, there is no certainty; there will always be some
person or group or class or people who will refuse, and legitimately so, the qualification of *historical* to such arbitrariness.
Moreover, what is the sense of history? We can only say that it
passes, follows, but no one can assert whether it progresses or re-
gresses without subjecting it to an absolute rule of measurement.
We already know that even civilizations are mortal, as Valéry

23. Cf. my article "L'attuale ambiguità dei diritti fondamentali,"
Rivista di diritto civile, 1977, pp. 225–42.

wrote, and Arnold Toynbee has shown us the mechanisms of this mortality. Humanity itself is not eternal; however, the only possible earthly certitude in the sense of history is that it leads inexorably to death.

There is no doubt that, despite this, the law is not left completely empty of its own essence as measure and consequently as rationality and dialogue. Its internal measure remains untouched: it is, in fact, not possible to imagine a juridical order without some precise correspondence and reciprocity of behaviors, some sort of continuity and regularity in human actions. Thus, the state of law in the form transmitted to us by nineteenth-century culture is a grandiose system of rules, a guarantee of behavioral regularity both on the part of the power and on the part of the people, and it is therefore a guarantee of the safety of life. But now the law does not reflect and does not even seek an external and a purposive measure founded on the objectivity of human structure. It openly presents itself, instead, as the rule devised (or imposed) by a given political will, entirely dependent upon it and its purpose; it does not seek any other foundation and justification. Detached from the objectivity of existence, it is exposed to the risk of being, as external measure, an exterior imposition; and, as purposive measure, ideology.

So juridical regulations and the state of law itself appear, to all who refuse to seek their essential foundations, to be extrinsic constructions, formalistic, cumbersome, and in any case, disputable in character and to be respected only for a long as it is convenient. Very seldom do they arouse the serious moral commitment that is rooted in the conviction that one's own duty toward oneself and society is accomplished by following the established norms. Often, very often, they appear to be pure imposition and violence: the will, deprived of its nexus with the universal, resolves itself into a hard order to all who are not identified with its particularity.

Herein lies the profound reason why the contemporary conception of the law does not constitute adequate insurance against violence; indeed, in the opinion of many, law plunges into violence that structurally is nonetheless its opposite. On the other hand, those theories that I have just criticized and that reduce law to force or only to rules on force (and therefore to exclusively activity-contra) are the logical consequence of the conception of law as *pure* will. And pure wills do not conduct dialogue nor do they agree: they threaten and impose upon each other. Their relation is that of a strong will to a weak one, as Nietzsche put it in all sincerety.[24]

24. Nietzsche, *Al di là del bene e del male*, aphorism 21 (Milan, 1968), p. 26.

Chapter 6

Why violence? II: the absolute subject

Crisis or reversal of values?

We have seen how the dependence (not always explicit though no less real) of today's conception of law on the metaphysics of subjectivity explains the fragility of the grandiose juridical construction, both theoretical and practical, of our times and, in particular, its difficulty in confronting violence on ideal grounds. A law whose foundation is a transient and even an arbitrary will rather than a solid defense against violence becomes a pretext for violence and risks offering a not totally unmotivated justification for it. But the adoption of the metaphysics of subjectivity as an interpretative key to today's violence has a hermeneutic value that goes much further than the clarification of the inadequacy of current law. Following that criterion, one may reach the very heart of our problem.

According to a judgment widespread both popularly and among scholars, today's violence is to be attributed to the *crisis of values* that characterizes our times. Whatever the assessment of it, negative or positive, there is general agreement on the *factuality* of such a crisis. And there is no doubt that when and where a crisis of values occurs, the conditions for violence are created. This truth has been recognized since the most remote times, in language different from ours but with very similar meaning, by the most diverse thinkers. From Plato to Machiavelli, from St. Augustine to Rousseau, the departure from "principles" is considered to be the cause of corruption, decadence, and conflicts. The principles to which these authors are referring are diverse, but the approach to the problem is the same. The analysis carried out by Durkheim renewed and clarified laudably a classical theme in terms of sociological determinateness. Anomie, the loss of or absence of reference to recognized values, doubtlessly creates a situation of disorientation (the needle of the moral compass has, so to speak, gone mad) in which violence finds no more obstacles.

All that is true but not sufficient. However broad the use of the term *crisis* may be (I, too, have used it in these pages), it is inadequate, for it corresponds only to a first level of observation and reflection. Really, there is seldom if ever a crisis due *only* to the departure from principles and to corruption nor is there any crisis resulting from the mere exhaustion or senescence of the cultural meanings of such principles. For the most part the effect of these negative motives, though present, is provoked or increased by the emergence of something new or renewed: the duration or the profundity of the crisis (and the difficulty of overcoming it) depend on the intensity of the novelty; the greater the novelty, the longer and more profound the crisis because of the number and importance of the broken lines that link the present to the past. But there is another even more delicate point to the whole question: only the value or disvalue of this "new" may clarify the sense of the crisis. This demonstrates that, besides a picture (always necessary) of the crisis, a critical analysis and discussion of the "new" that provokes or aggravates it is indispensable. It is true that today the conviction that "new" is synonymous with "good" and "just" is very diffuse, so every crisis would be positive. But this is an attitude as fideistic, acritical, and unjustified as the opposite conviction that "good" and "just" are only "the past." In short, as we cannot ascertain the dimension of the crisis without a precise comprehension of the extension of the "new," so we cannot assert its positivity or negativity without an examination of the value of the "new."

In regard to the problem of violence, the question is determinant. In fact, a violence from *pure and simple* anomie (from *pure and simple* crisis of decline) is doubtless possible but probably of short duration, desultory, in relation to which the classical call "to go back to the origins" (so dear even to Machiavelli) can be sufficient. In any case, in such a hypothesis there is no room for the exaltation of violence; since no society can survive on principle in general anomie, the violence generated by anomie can reveal itself to be analytically comprehensible but certainly not acceptable to either intellective or moral conscience. So the violence of which we all talk, today's violence, in which the announcement of and the hope for the "new" occupy a determinant place, is not diagnosable as violence springing from *pure* anomie, a *pure* crisis of values. The reference to the metaphysics of subjectivity helps us understand that the foundation of these phenomena (anomie and crisis) is definitely an active moment, a new evaluative proposal. As Max Scheler perfectly understood, we are faced by a *reversal* of values.

The question is not one of more or less intellectualistically appropriate terms but one of substance: while (pure) anomie is a phenomenon of dereliction—and therefore of passive contrast between the old and the new—the reversal is a phenomenon of confrontation, of active contrast. In this second situation, the "going back to original principles" cannot consist in a mere operation of (stimulating or persevering) reeducation. It demands something more: a tight critical examination of the actual consistency and value of the new principles.

What provokes a crisis, as I said, is the reversal of values. Some easily perceptible examples will suffice. I shall consider first of all the area of social values. Here (I give a first example) the value, which until some time ago was considered to be supreme, is in crisis; I mean honesty, unselfishness in public administration, the so-called sense of the state in political activity. Today administration and the state are no longer perceived as institutional ex-

pressions of the community to which one owes generous dedica-
tion and scrupulous service but as centers of power to be occupied
for personal or group interests, essential instruments for the purpose of manipulating opinions and consensus. Moreover, if in the
last century the main path to public influence was through private
wealth (as it still is in the United States), today, on the contrary, it
is in fact public influence that produces private wealth. This appears in a particularly significant manner in the socialist regimes,
where those who hold power established themselves as an eco-
nomically privileged "new class" thanks to their political position, as Milovan Djilas demonstrated. This is not a question of
corruption: profiteers, arrivistes, Machiavellians of high and low
ranks have always existed; evil is certainly not a novelty. Nor is it
due only to the change in the economic infrastructure of society,
even if this has a notable importance. Underneath is something
more profound.

It is the very idea of *res publica*, of common good (the idea that
structures public life from its foundation) that has lost its value
and is rejected or allowed to fall. Its place is taken by the conception of politics as pure power, which is theorized with undisturbed certainty: a can-do that *is value in itself*, since it is the
expression of man's active capacity in which today many perceive
his specific essence and which therefore does not and cannot encounter any ideal limit except, in point of fact, that of its own
power. This intellectual position, whether consciously or not, has
its foundation (and somehow finds the clarification of its profound meaning) in the Nietzschean thesis according to which the
value of man rests with his power. Not coincidentally is Nietzsche
explicit in the condemnation of the idea of the common good:
"'Good' is no longer good if it is on the lips of the neighbor.
And could there ever exist a 'common good'! The word is self-
contradictory: that which can be in common always has very little
value." And, more emphatically: "'General welfare' is not an
ideal, a goal, a somehow graspable concept, but only an emetic." [1]
If man is totally resolved into his own praxis, and consequently

1. *Al di là del bene e del male*, aphorisms 43 and 228, pp. 48, 137.

into his own power, it is completely logical that politics is reduced to mere power. And if this is politics—a can-do according to power—it is not surprising that it is the field for a ruthless and even pitiless game whose stake is power, free can-do.

Let us consider as a second example one of the most ordinary, apparently banal, daily events of our relational life: road traffic. Very few concern themselves with others and fewer than ever with orderly traffic, both of which would be advantageous to all. Whether in a hurry or interested in chatting with his automobile companion, everyone drives his car as he pleases and according to his own interests, leaves it where it is convenient for him; others only hinder and obstruct him to the point of arousing a fit of violence in him. In this case too, what counts is the self, which is bolstered and made confident by the mechanical device at his disposal and with which, very often, he identifies through a fancied assimilation of the motor's power and the power of his personality.

A third example is chosen from the area of sexual life. The idea (or the slogan) of the "public use of the private," that is, the negation of decency, is arrogantly opposed to those who speak with reprobation of a crisis in decency. The question of decency is a complex one in which self-respect, as the custodian of one's own privacy, and the respect of others' privacy are inseparably intertwined: a personal value is intertwined with an interpersonal value so that the sociality of the relation is based on reciprocal respect. From Plato—remember the very keen relationship between decency and justice enunciated in the *Protagoras*—to Vico, from the passages on the education of women in Rousseau's *Émile* to Max Scheler's reflection there is an entire tradition of philosophers, and not only of moralists, who emphasize the social value and the significance of civilized decency. Its negation does not carry with it only, as one may believe or pretend to believe, freer and more genuine sexual habits but it actualizes the integral reduction of personality to bodily praxis, in the ostentation *ad libitum* (and therefore according to power) of the body and its acts. The bodily praxis becomes the rule and the culmination of the arbitrariness and praxistic power of the individual. In this desolate *nudité humaine*, the personality is dissolved into the occasional and stimulated (and therefore passive) impulsion of the body; life it-self runs a mortal risk, as Jean Brun clearly pointed out.[2]

But whatever the personal outcome of the end of decency, it is certain that the publicizing of this very private aspect of the "private" is the result of a conception according to which the self, in the most individualized determinateness of its praxis (the bodily, to be exact), is assumed to be the supreme value to whose arbitrariness other values must passively subordinate themselves. As I have tried to show elsewhere,[3] we are confronted with a reversal of the usual way of understanding the relation between public and private: the private no longer wants to be protected in its privacy from the intrusion of the public; it wants, instead, to impose publicly on everyone the absolute arbitrariness of its own will, to receive public recognition (and, if necessary, public assistance) of the sovereignty of its own doing. It is the private itself that vindicates its own immediate public authority. In this perspective, the demand for "a free and publicly financed" abortion constitutes the extreme imposition upon the public of a private will and sentiment, at the cost of the life of another innocent and defenseless human being.[4] The law would thus be supposed to sanction the supremacy of the self over the social and interpersonal relation (and over responsibility).

I have chosen the above examples—of diverse importance but of equal meaning—in order to offer a sort of orientation for the ground on which the rise of the new fundamental value of the self manifests itself in many other ways. Doubtless, in such examples a crisis of values is evident: honesty, solidarity, and respect for others appear discredited and abandoned. But it would be a vain undertaking to try to reestablish them through a moral reeducation, if this were not based on the critical investigation of what

2. In the cited book, *La nudité humaine* (Paris, 1973).

3. In my article, "La sexualité en tant que dernier mythe politique," *Res Publica*, 17 (1975): 357–66.

4. For an illuminating cultural analysis of the question, see L. Lombardi Vallauri, *Abortismo libertario e sadismo* (Milan, 1976).

determined the crisis. We are faced by the proposal of a different conception of man—that of the self as praxis—and therefore of a different value: that of the self as power. This is a real reversal, whose result is that the individual becomes blameless while the reponsibility falls entirely on society. Once again it is Nietzsche who clarifies the situation: it is enough to recall his constant and radical repudiation of the morality based on the love for one's fellow man (the most solid foundation of sociability) and his imperious vindication of the supremacy of power, pushed as far as the identification of it with the joyful earthliness of the body[5] (but is it joyful, perhaps, only because it has not experienced suffering and decay?).

The metaphysics of subjectivity, then, is perceived as the exaltation of the most private self. But at the opposite extreme in radical antithesis stands the loss of value of this very self. In today's mass man, or the man forced into gregariousness, the values of public and private freedom, responsibility, and individual courage have entered a state of crisis. In a purely quantitative democracy, the single individual does not count for anything; in a collectivistic regime, individuality is the great enemy. In the mass media civilization, the individual is dissolved into the banal conformity of groups, languages, and stereotyped judgments; the voice of those who have no access to the collective instrument of diffusion remains unheard in the sense that it is not listened to and its eccentricity makes it unacceptable.

The phenomenology and the desolate poverty of the mass man, of the "lonely crowd," has been described too many times for me to dwell on it. It is enough to recall one more case, which is significant because it is intertwined with the opposite tendency toward the arrogance of the self: that of the loss of the sense of privacy. If, as I have just pointed out, privacy is on the one hand displayed and imposed on the public, publicized as the ultimate manifestation of the supremacy of the self, on the other it is con-

5. Cf. Nietzsche, *Cosí parlò Zarathustra* "Dei dispregiatori del corpo" [The scorners of the body], 1:34–36.

tinuously violated under the pretext of the public's right to information. A misunderstood right to ever more invasive chronicles (too often malicious if not discrediting) overcomes every defense of privacy. Often such invasions are ambiguously demanded by those who should defend themselves against them: this is a definite sign of the loss of the sense of self, since self-consciousness is felt only if one's name is on everyone's lips, only if one has a *public image*, built (perhaps by others) on the emptiness of his own personality in order to correspond to the standardized opinion of others in whose mirror only can one find himself. And how many images one has to make and unmake of oneself to keep up with the changes in public opinion! The individual disappears under the mobile pressure of praxis, even if in this case it is the praxis of an alien and faceless crowd.

All custody or manifestation of individuality is then negated, not only in fact but also in principle, since the individual is reduced to a pure negativity, a pure egoism. Perhaps Rousseau, better than any other modern thinker, gave an exemplary expression to this feeling. It is necessary, he wrote, to denature man; it is necessary that everyone renounce all of his personal rights in order to enjoy only those allowed by the "general will," since the individual is only a "fraction" of the social "whole" and therefore draws his human significance and value from being part of that "whole."[6] The new value is consequently the totality—an ambiguous, multifaceted concept, whose fortune has been increasing from Rousseau to Hegel and Marx.

However, this assumption of the social "whole" as a fundamental value, unless proved unwarranted, implicitly presupposes a two-faceted theoretical process. In one sense, in fact, we will have a conceptual entification of the "whole," thanks to its conspicuous appearance in history. But is it not possible that only this abstract entity is the author of history, which is the vicissitude of concrete men? In the other sense, the reality of personal conscience is symmetrically negated and personal conscience is re-

6. Cf. *Émile*, in *Œuvres complètes*, Pléiade edition, 4: 249.

duced to an epiphenomenon of social and material living conditions, by which it would be determined and thus held as a passive refraction of the collective conscience. But, in turn, the "whole" so constructed may demonstrate itself to be real (not a mere intellectualistic abstraction) only on condition that the triumph or imposition of a rigorously collective praxis is realized, which implies the actual silencing of the personal conscience. The value of the "whole" depends, therefore, on the effectiveness of the praxis that imposes it. Consequently, every action by the individual is looked upon with suspicion and whenever it is autonomous, it is made culpable as the action of an "enemy of the people," to use the title of Ibsen's well-known drama. Every meritorious act by the individual is, instead, attributed to society (or to its enlightened officials), whose wise directives the individual dutifully observes. The mass consciousness is the ultimate but necessary consequence of this reversal of values that, by depriving the personal conscience of any meaning, replaces the responsible freedom of the individual with the anonymous sovereignty of the "whole." Society thus becomes the new "subject" that measures the world, positing itself as the rule, and proclaims itself the foundation and the exclusive criterion of judgment of men's concrete life, scorning individuality as a mere transitory appearance.[7]

The crisis that is widely noticed is, therefore, the external but widespread manifestation of this dual process of the reversal of values. On the one side, we exalt, in contrast to the value of sociability, the value of an *I* of fantasized innocence and power, conceivable only if one ignores and denies the reasons and the responsibilities of the living-together. On the other side, we propose, against the value of individuality, the value of a *We* of mythical existence and perfection, conceivable only if one ignores or denies the humanity of the individual and the creative freedom of the *I*. In this process of reversal, we have unity on the one hand and anti-

7. One is thus trying to compensate the frustration produced by the immanentistic negation of the immortality of the individual, transferring such an immortality to the social "whole."

nomy on the other; this is the reason for my speaking of a *dual* process and not of *two* separate processes. In fact, we have unity because both positions possess the essential characteristic of *absolutization* of the subject (either individual or collective); both are therefore concomitantly opposed to the usual tables of values that do not view the individual and society as antagonists, and more profoundly, to those conceptions of the world for which the subject is not the founding (and thus exclusive) principle of reality. We have, on the other hand, an *internal* antinomy in that process, since obviously the affirmation of the primacy of the *I* is definitely opposed to the affirmation of the primacy of the *We*, and conversely.

There is, therefore, at the root of the crisis, a contrast of values that, due to its complexity, complicates and multiplies the reasons for antagonism and conflict. We must also keep in mind, moreover, that both the one and the other of the new proposed fundamental values can free themselves of mythicization or fantastication only to the extent that they succeed in embodying themselves in a real praxis, capable of imposing each value on the opposite values. Therefore, praxis is no longer justified by the value, but value is to be based (if it wants to become reality) on praxis, which is self-justified. Now if it is true that one gets out of fantastication and dream through praxis, it is equally true that a praxis that is its own principle is resolved into a pure exercise of power. The primary and more obvious cultural explanation for today's violence lies in this situation of open and radical contraposition of values, whose solution is entrusted to praxis. As long as such a conflict between nonmediated values prolongs itself, violence will find in it the most favorable conditions for its explosion and for its lasting endemic diffusion.

The scissions of existential dialectic

The flourishing of violence can, then, be traced back first to the conflictual reversal of the values that is due to the absoluteness of the subject, both individual and collective, in which, in my opinion, the metaphysics of subjectivity consists. We must now reflect

on this absolutization. It is, in fact, articulated in a series of abso-
lutizations, which constitute as many scissions of the delicate dialectic nexuses typical of existence. I shall briefly point out the
most important ones.

THE NEXUS LIBERTY-RESPECT

Liberty is certainly a good, a value inherent in man as such. Thus,
because of its quality of value inherent in the essence[8] and not in
the accidentality of man, liberty is everyone's legitimate aspiration. We can also apply to liberty the "qualifier of universalization" of which the logicians speak, so that liberty must be recognized in or attributed to *everyone*. But a problem arises here: is it
possible to apply to liberty—or to any other value[9]—not only the
qualifier of universalization but also *together with it* that which I
call by analogy the "qualifier of absolutization," so that one may
have *all* conceivable liberty? In the case of the unified application
of the two qualifiers, *everyone* should enjoy *all* conceivable liberty.
But this is clearly impossible: if I enjoy *all* liberty, if I am free to
do whatever I want, the Other is not. We are then faced by an
alternative: either we apply the qualifier of universalization—and
thus *everyone* has a limited freedom—or we apply the qualifier of
absolutization and thus *all* freedom is allowed to a *limited* number
of subjects: *tertium non datur* [there is no third alternative].

Now, the metaphysics of subjectivity is obliged to choose the
second solution: in fact, if the subject (individual or collective) is
the absolute principle or the measure of value, its freedom cannot
be anything but absolute. The other individual or community,
therefore, cannot help but appear to him as the obstacle to his

8. Historical or ontological? I shall examine this point further
on. For the moment it suffices to observe that one can believe the historicity of man and nevertheless think that liberty is *today* the patrimony of the historical conscience of humanity.

9. V. Mathieu has brilliantly utilized this criterion in the case of
equality: cf. his article, "L'eguaglianza giuridica" [Juridical equality]
in *Rivista internazionale della filosofia del diritto*, 54 (1977), pp. 18–26.

freedom, to his being-himself. Sartre has insisted often (and in full consistency with his premises) on the total, limiting, and even "nauseating" unintelligibility of the Other—the Other whose mere presence suffices to prevent the world from belonging to me. (But under what title, in which way do I vindicate it or make it *mine?* These are pure intellectualistic artifices.) Therefore, Sartre could utter in *Huis clos* the well-known phrase: "*L'enfer c'est les autres*"; before Sartre, in a similar vein, Malraux had Kyo, the protagonist of his *La condition humaine*, say, in a nighttime soliloquy: "*Les hommes ne sont pas mes semblables, ils sont ceux qui me regardent et me jugent.*" (At night, when man indulges in oneiric fantastication: "*Comme si sa pensée n'eût plus été faite pour la lumière,*" as Malraux himself recognizes.)

This opaque extraneousness of the Other—his cold judgment of me—is the negation of my freedom as a self-founded subject and is therefore my hell: the Other must then be denied so that I may acquire my total liberty. This not only breaks the secondary dialectical nexus that unites liberty and authority—to which we usually direct our attention—but also and more profoundly, it breaks the primary and positive dialectic nexus between liberty and respect. According to a current opinion, to universalize freedom it suffices that the freedom of one stop where the freedom of another begins. This is a fallacious opinion: as Spinoza (and after him Nietzsche) saw clearly, this stopping point is not determined by freedom but by the exhaustion of the power of the subject or by its clash with the power of the Other. The only condition for the universalization of freedom (extended to everyone, but for this very reason limited) is respect, since my respect for the Other makes me conscious of the legitimacy of his freedom and so of the dutiful limits of mine. Therefore, if this nexus is broken, there is indeed total liberty, but only for those who are powerful; for others there is only serfdom. We are in this case in the presence of a *negative* dialectic, of an antinomy of freedoms, incapable of a synthesis that makes them simultaneously possible. The Other is not to be respected; he is reduced to raw material, to a passive object of the will of the free subject. So violence is misrepresented as the exercise of freedom, and under a different name it becomes free to unleash itself.

THE NEXUS MOVEMENT–DURATION

Liberty implies movement. This is evident: one is not completely free when impeded in one's movements. Freedom of movement does not concern only spatial mobility (to go wherever you wish or exercise your own activity wherever you please) but also social mobility, which overcomes the closed sociological-cultural or institutional, preconstituted boundaries of classes. Not coincidentally is this double possibility of movement considered a sign of the greater freedom acquired by today's man as compared to the materially static and compartmentalized life of the past. Doubtless one can be internally free (mobile) even when in jail or immobilized by sickness providing one spiritually transcends the situation, which in such a case can even become the dialectic condition for achieving freedom. The enclosure within the "hedgerow" for Leopardi or within the barbed wire of the Gulag for Solzhenitsyn opens the way to the comprehension of the infinite or of the authentic meaning of freedom. But this is true for the exceptional individual and not in all of the moments of even his existence. In any event, it is indispensable that the impediment to physical movement be cancelled by the freedom of the movement of ideas, because if this freedom is hindered, the only possible witness to the inner movement is God, certainly not history or the Others, who can conceive only the visible or the audible. Therefore, the recent charters of man's rights justly register among the liberties those of moving and of allowing his own ideas to circulate.

Movement is thus the expression of freedom in relation to the world surrounding us—things, persons, society. However, deeper within us, the movement (or change) is freeedom also in relation to oneself. He who is incapable or unwilling ever to change in and by himself his ideas, opinions, and habits exists as a passive, not a free subject *(subjectum,* subjected). He is his own prisoner to the point of being an automaton whose movements are rigorously determined. In his continuous and tormented vindication of absolute freedom for the future superman, Nietzsche pushed to the extreme the exigency of liberty of movement. It is not enough for him to liberate the soul "from any obedience, reverence, and subjection to others," he wants to be able to change even in relation to himself. "I am the *continuous, necessary overcoming of myself*," life had confessed to Zarathustra; so he declared that he would "be nothing but struggle and *becoming* and purpose and *contradiction* of purposes." [10]

In this double sense (toward others and toward self), the movement-change is implicit in the idea and in the reality of freedom. But as the absolutization of the subject implies the absolutization of freedom, so the absolutization of freedom implies that of movement. The dialectical nexus between movement and duration is split. And the consequences of such splitting are disastrous: once more life is abandoned to the capricious game of the praxis of power and of violence.

In relation to the surrounding world, the absolutization of the movement of the individual subject brings about the negation of *historical memory*, of that lasting continuity that translates itself into institutions in the broadest sense of the word: juridical-political, cultural, linguistic institutions. And since these are present in real life and consequently through their duration prevent the total mobility of the subject, they are deprived of their human character and reduced to encumbering material things. Thus, the hatred for institutions as such emerges, together with the justification of every violence against them, and goes as far as to demand their complete and definitive elimination, since every institution, every historical memory would be an unjustified limitation of the possibility of movement. To verify what I have said there is no need to have recourse to the neoanarchical turbulence with which today's life abounds. It is enough to remember the futurist call for the destruction of the institution of language itself in the name of the "freedom of words" and the frenzy of movement.

10. Cf. Nietzsche, *Così parlo Zarathustra*, 3 : 271 and 2: 139. (The first italic is in the text, the second is mine—SC.)

But the individual deprived of historical memory is condemned to lose the sense of belonging to a political but above all a spiritual fatherland: it is the *déracinement* criticized by Weil. He thus falls into the desolate estrangement of the legend's wandering Jew, out of his element everywhere and therefore unable to find anywhere a familiar and friendly face or thing.

In the case of the collective subject, the absolute freedom of movement that it claims for itself in history has a dual effect. On the one hand, it institutionalizes the rivalry among collective subjects, suppressing in it the character of evil and sparing it from any criterion of judgment that is not fact. The movement of history, its meaning, is determined from that collective subject (people, race, class, culture) that is shown by facts to be more powerful: if this power must be elicited through warlike or revolutionary violence, it will be painful but inevitable. On the other hand, the absolute freedom of movement of the collective subject implies that every autonomous movement-change of the individual loses all values and must thus be blocked. In their movement, revolutions not only eliminate their own adversaries but they devour their own makers. Since the epoch of revolutions began, not one of them has been an exception to this: from the French Revolution to the Chinese Revolution the phenomenon is constant and there is a reason. Being a praxis that aims to engage the movement of history on a completely new road (never tried before), the revolution can prove the goodness of that new road only by opening it through a compact collective march, in respect to which every individual path is a deviation. Therefore, the mobility of the collective subject is guaranteed by the immobility of the concentration camp, the political insane asylum, or death for the dissenter. But can we have a historical memory without the work of individuals, without their feeling it as their own, as a conjoined but personal construction?

The consequences are no less serious for the individual who breaks the dialectical nexus between his own change and his own duration, absolutizing the former. In such a case, that which is lost is not only historical memory but the memory of self, the consciousness of one's own continuing identity in time. The subject, identifying himself with the precise coincidence of change and temporal instant, burns at every moment his own personality, falling into that radical estrangement (the *Heimatlosigkeit* of Heidegger) that deprives him of his own being. Thus his most intimate consistency, his belonging to himself, is dissolved into that wandering of *bateau ivre* whose ultimate way out is the desire to smash itself: "*Oh! que ma quille éclate,*" declares Rimbaud. The profound and illuminating meaning of the Christian conception of life as a journey (toward a goal! present in the interiority and yet transcendent) is lost in a journey (a life) without meaning or beyond any meaning in the domain of hallucination: is not perhaps the memory–destructive hallucination induced by drugs called "trip" by antonomasia? Jean Brun wrote very penetratingly on this subject, and he was above all able to grasp that singular reversal by which the individual, in absolutizing himself ("*repu de lui-même*"), sinks into an "emptiness from which no individuality could ever reemerge" and consequently gives himself up to the frenzy of the alienating journey.[11] Violence against historical memory, violence against oneself up to the point of destruction: separated from duration, movement leads to these results. In truth, only the synthesis with duration (shadow and terrestrial image of the eternal) makes it possible that the change not be negation and self-destruction, but development to the fullness of one's own being.

THE NEXUS HISTORY–BEING

The nexuses between liberty and respect and between movement and duration are united in the nexus between history and being. In fact, on the one side it appears evident that liberty and movement are implicated in the concept and effectiveness of history; on the other, there is no respect, as the condition of freedom, if not of an entity that really *is*, just as duration (that is, the condition of the nondispersiveness of movement) is continuity and permanence of *being*. Consequently, the scissions noted above are

11. *Les vagabonds de l'Occident*, p. 27 and passim.

brought together in the scission of history from being and in the coherent absolutization of the former. Consider the emblematic assertion of Ortega y Gasset: "Man has no nature, but has . . . history." [12] That man is a historical entity is certain and obvious: it is his inherent deficiency that imperiously demands—at the urging of a profound need for plenitude—movement and liberty, that is, history.

However, the historicity of man pushed to its limit ends in Sartre's well-known thesis: "Existence precedes essence"; it means, in unequivocal terms, that essence is the product of existence. And since it seems to me that an existence that produces essence cannot be understood as anything other than *action*, then it must be *action* that gives origin to or creates *being*. And in a certain sense this is true: the book that I publish, the pen with which I write, *are* here because they were previously *made*. But this is the world in which objects are produced: would the *self-development* of man then be a self-creation similar to that of objects? Let us not dismiss this question as irrelevant or mystifying by replying that man in his self-creation would make any object but himself: that is, an active subject that manifests and develops itself in its own activity. I do not deny this at all, but this is not the point. Creative existence is particularity: my activity belongs to me and not to someone else; it is then a particular activity that can bring about only a particular fact. The essence produced by existence is therefore also a particularity like that which produces it: and in fact it is *my* essence. This means that men, being different among themselves because of their particular existence, no longer possess a common essence for communicating among themselves: such an essence, too, is dissolved in the particularity inherent in the product of a particular activity, which opens an insurmountable abyss between man and man. Life comes to present itself as a crossing, clashing, and repelling of "monads" incapable of communicating, each of which is for the other simply an object that is due no

12. *Historia como sistema*, in *Obras completas* (Madrid, 1950–52) 6:41. Published in English as *History as a System and Other Essays Toward a Philosophy of History* (New York, 1961).

respect. In short, by positing existence as prior to essence, it *is believed* that one reaches the summit of subjectivity as self-possession, but in reality we surrender the ones to the others reciprocally, as objects bereft of human meaning. In the last analysis, indeed, we are dissolved, since an existence that precedes the essence is no longer *one*, but it is disintegrated into its multiple and various empirical acts.

One might say that this is a very unusual presentation of the meaning of history, which differs particularly from that of historians. The observation is correct precisely because the history of the historians is not absolutized and is therefore not an activity that, on the one hand, would ignore the precedence of something that *is* and, on the other, would produce only incommunicable and ephemeral facts. The historicity of which the historians speak (and with them many historicist philosophers) is not at all movement without duration or action without memory. For this reason Nietzsche, the absolutizer par excellence of the will and the movement of the subject, fiercely attacks *this* history. Since his *Use and Abuse of History* (1874), devoted to this problem, he presents the memory consigned to history as the main obstacle to free action. "Every action demands oblivion," he wrote at that time; therefore Zarathustra will teach oblivion and will proclaim that every true creator "must be first of all a destroyer."[13] The negation of historicity as duration and memory, which make real the mobility and liberty of the subject, is then the necessary condition for attaining the absolute historicity of the subject. Not by coincidence does Nietzsche laud the historiography that *destroys*, and he himself, through a similar fanciful historical analysis (the "genealogy of morals"), thinks that he has destroyed the lasting bond of morality, of the *you ought*.

But in this absolutization of history separated from being, this latter disappears not only as an anthropological essence but also as a subjective being, since the individual will, in order to attain total freedom (that of the superman) is forced to the unconditional acceptance of temporal events. In fact, if the oblivion or the

13. *Così parlo Zarathustra*, "The Victory upon Oneself," 2: 140.

destruction of the past (and of the present) is the condition for the liberation of the will, it is because "the will is not able to will backward," but it inevitably clashes with the objectivity of the "it was," of the "already-happened." Consequently, Nietzsche—in the face of this "stone which the will cannot roll"—is forced to conclude: "All 'it was' is a fragment, a riddle, a fearful chance— until the creating will saith thereto: 'But thus do I will it! Thus shall I will it!'"[14] This is for Nietzsche the "redemption": a will that wants to liberate itself from the objectivity of the "it was" and from the mysteriousness of the things-to-come can do nothing but accept them unconditionally, declaring that it wanted them as they were and will be. There is no ambiguity in the terms or the sophistication of the arguments that may lead to a change of meaning of this decisive text. If man pursues the dream of his own ever-new presence (Faust's eternal youth), he is in reality abandoned to the dominant extraneousness of fleeing time. Therefore, the total liberation of the will through the absolutization of the historical movement is self-refuted: the will is forced to want all that is produced in time, estranging itself in an inactive passivity from which it attempts to save itself by trusting in the mythical hope of finding itself in the eternal cyclical return of the equal.

The dizziness of subjectivity and possibility

Let us summarize. The metaphysics of subjectivity contains all the theoretical-practical tendencies of which I have just spoken and perhaps still more. As we have seen, they follow a common itinerary. First they isolate and then absolutize the facts of experience or undeniable exigencies of existence—who could deny reality and value to liberty, movement, history?—in the conviction that they thus ensure full development and self-possession in the subject. But for this very reason these tendencies end up with the opposite result. From the theoretical point of view, in fact, they are self-refuted, since in the separation-absolutization freedom

14. Ibid., 2: 171, 172.

reverses itself to reification, movement to failure, history to disintegration or passivity. From the practical point of view they provoke an unredeemable violence and, thus, the ultimate destruction of the subject itself. This appears to be the nihilistic destiny, which is marked by its refusal of a *positive* dialectic, that is, the dialectic that does not bring about the incurable conflict originating from the antinomies, but which in itself requires the existential synthesis.

Such a singular nihilistic outcome of the Promethean ambition deserves further study. A careful look at them shows that the various particular scissions, through which the (individual or collective) subject absolutizes itself as the principle and measure of itself and the world, are rooted and find their explanation in something more profound than the refusal of the existential dialectical nexuses. They originate, in fact, in the oblivion of that fundamental ontological relationship to which I have referred here and there in the preceding chapters, which is constitutive of the human structure and therefore of the very modes of existence. In the concrete and permanent reality of life, there is no place for a self-founded and self-reflecting subject, be it the *I* or the *We*, which are both constructed in their impermeable aseity through a sort of hypostatizing *transfert* dichotomizing that which is united. The ontological primary fact of life (and not only of human life) is, instead, the relationship "I-with-the-Other."

It is a multilevel relationship: with (inorganic and organic) nature, with other men, with the supreme *Alter* (and also *Idem*) that is God.[15] Insofar as our being is a "being-in-the-world," to quote Heidegger, the *I* is situated at the point of intersection of an innumerable series of relationships: biological, affective, cultural, social, spiritual. The ontological relation expresses, in a synthetic manner, the reality (and necessity) of these relations and confers upon them a foundation and a sense. Consequently, as I have written on other occasions, the *I is* to the extent that it *is-in-*

15. This last relation, which is a classical theme of Christian thought, has been reproposed with autonomous vigor by the phenomenology of the sacred: think of R. Otto or of Van der Leeuw.

relation, and is self-conscious to the extent that it is perceived as *I-in-relation*.[16] The consciousness of the relation as the foundation of individuality takes away from individuality every subjectivistic and Promethean character: the more we deepen our living-together the more we are ourselves. And in this way we prevent the hypostatization of an abstract *We:* the *we* will be, instead, the result of the encounter of individualities conscious of their relationship. The relation is, therefore, the very condition of life and consciousness, for outside it there is only nothingness and death.

In the interhuman relation certainly every individual is different from any other, but each is always *like me*, partaking of the same being, indeed of the very being that I am. Since he does not identify himself with me, he may represent a limit, an obstacle to my activity; but his difference-participation makes him dialectically equally indispensable to the development of my very *I*, that in itself is structurally defective, lacking, incomplete. To recognize the Other is then the indispensable premise for deeply understanding oneself, one's own incompleteness, and the request for help and friendship that springs from the depth of our being. With this recognition, the road to an effective and authentic self-development is opened to the individual, who is the irreplaceable protagonist of the human adventure.

In fact, in light of the ontological relation, the Other appears as an indispensable *partner* in all of human life: from being to existence and beyond this to another life. Perhaps one can live without others' memory, but certainly there is no terrestrial survival; without the Other that is God, resurrection and eternal life is unthinkable. In the consciousness of the ontological relation, reciprocal respect finds a sure foundation, which does not depend upon the fluctuating contingence of situations, feelings, or utility but upon the full comprehension of its own structural relational

16. Cf. My *Itinerari esistenziali del diritto* (Naples, 1972), p. 61ff. P. Piovani expressed it very well: "L'esistere è coesistere: non c'è esistenza che non sia coesistenza" [To exist is to co-exist: there is no existence which is not co-existence] (*Principi di una filosofia morale* [Naples, 1972], p. 41; cf. p. 157ff).

character. The liberty for all is thus founded, everyone being saved in principle from the reification to which he is doomed by refusing respect. The ontological relation constitutes, moreover, the criterion of discernment of the objective rule (that is, non-arbitrary, nonsubjectively exclusivistic) of behavior, since both terms of the relation are equally necessary to life. Therefore, the subjectivity (liberty, movement, history) of man is not legitimately allowed to prevaricate on the subjectivity (liberty, movement, history) of the Other, for both subjectivities are open to dialogue, whose seriousness is guaranteed by reference to a common measure. In short, in the recognition of the individual relation we respect the being that we are and, therefore, life as it is structurally, and we find a valid criterion for the refusal of violence in favor of a commitment to mutual understanding and co-operation, that is, to life together.

Now, because of its process of absolutization, the metaphysics of subjectivity implies the disregard or rupture of the ontological relation, since it denies the Other (nature, man, God) the very quality of structural *partner* in existence. We have thus found ourselves in the *dizziness of subjectivity*, which mirrors itself with self-complacency and refuses limitations; therefore, when it is not weakened by the illusion of dream, it breaks loose into the boundlessness of its desires—think of the vindication of the "*libération du désire*" by André Breton,[17] which is now on everyone's lips—and of the arrogance of the will. The Other, excluded from the participation in my own being and, therefore, from dialogue and no longer worthy of respect, is reduced either to raw material, a passive object of my calculating and dominating will, or to a non-redeemable enemy. No longer my like, he is really my hell, the source and the target of a hatred that in reality is fueled by the innumerable defeats and frustrations of which the subject itself is the cause because it cut itself off from its indispensable *partner*.

In this dizziness of subjectivity, which refuses every objective rule, today's violence finds its most profound cultural explana-

17. On this see A. del Noce, "Interpretazione filosofica del surrealismo," *Rivista di Estetica* 10 (1965), pp. 22–54.

tion. From the will to power to the liberation of desires, the metaphysics of subjectivity offers the subtlest justifications for saving the structural characteristics of violence (unruliness, passionality, depersonalization of the Other, lack of dialogue) from the condemning judgment that considers them the source of destruction. Such metaphysics instead presents these characteristics as coherent manifestations of a subject that seeks and wants only itself and that is satisfied only with itself. This is the explanation of that which, as I noted in the first chapter, is really *new* in today's violence: its exaltation. But if it is true that the ontological relation is the very way in which real life is constituted, its negation does not imply at all the liberation of the *I*, but its destruction. Not coincidentally do the theory and praxis that forget this relation appear destined to find nothingness and to cause death (to themselves and others).[18]

However, despite these clearly catastrophic results, the dizziness of subjectivity is there; indeed, it is so diffused as to characterize a time in our own history not yet closed. What does prevent it, then, from showing its face for the deceptive fiction it is? I believe that the extraordinary power of transformation acquired by man over nature through science and technology is the answer. The dominance over nature, according to an ancient and always deceptive dream of man, has appeared as definitively achieved with the advent of the technological age. I shall not repeat what I said elsewhere, particularly in my *Sfida tecnologica* [Technological challenge] and in my *L'uomo tolemaico* [The Ptolemaic man]. It suffices here to say that from the domination over the nature of things we have been moving also to the domination over the nature of man through biochemical and psychical intervention and prospective genetic engineering. The boundaries of the possible are so widened as to seem nonexistent. The dizziness of subjectivity has been thus acquiring credibility because it rests on the apparently solid basis of the domination of man over nature.

18. The case of Sartre is emblematic: in *L'être et le néant* he theorizes the encounter with nothingness and in *Le Diable et le bon Dieu* the realization of oneself through the death of the Other.

Henri de Saint-Simon once predicted a happy and peaceful humanity living in abundance and so liberated from the secret impulse of man to dominate man. And Marx followed in his footsteps. The subject as a measure of itself, liberated from every co-existential limit and free in all its desires, seems, therefore, to find a real basis for the self-complacency of man becoming a measure of the cosmos and capable of composing its elements according to his own desires and interests.

But the widening of possibility has also produced a dizziness whose climax for man is not liberation at all, but death. Everyone already knows that the domination over nature—violence over nature's structures of existence—has made real and put into the hands of man for the first time in history the ultimate possibility of final catastrophe in the world, whether nuclear or ecological. It is an apocalypse without resurrection. The confidence of Saint-Simon and Marx that violence discharged on nature rather than on other men is ultimately beneficial appears, therefore, to be pure illusion. More acute than they, Nietzsche understood it when he wrote: "He who with his knowledge throws nature into the abyss of nothingness must experience on himself also the dissolution of nature."[19] Violence cannot be saved only by changing its target, since its structure and meaning, which are characterized by disproportion and destructiveness, remain unchanged. The changing of target does nothing but dress it with false innocence. Therefore, the encounter of a possibility and a subjectivity, both thought to be unlimited, makes their respective destructive powers even more impending and threatening. One cannot eliminate a dizziness with another dizziness.

19. Nietzsche, *La nascita della tragedia*, par. 9.

Epilogue

What we have been saying should induce reflection on the aporias of the metaphysics of subjectivity, which developed according to its own principles, refuted itself, and produced such devastating dizzinesses. In order to free oneself from this negative outcome, then, is it necessary to turn again to the metaphysics of being? I think so, but the subject goes beyond the purpose of these pages, the more so since the possible expressions of the metaphysics of being are many, although homogeneous in their inspiration. However, I believe it indispensable to indicate two of my convictions on this matter.

First, this return to the metaphysics of being cannot avoid implicating the critical consciousness, the close discernment of "what is living and what is dead," of what is valid and what is negative in such a metaphysics, which certainly did not form itself through a mere error or pure arrogance. Therefore, the return to it is not at all an *antimodern* one (even if we should admit, which we do not, that the whole of modernity is expressed in the metaphysics of subjectivity), but a *postmodern* one that is critically en-riched with the whole experience of recent thought. It is in this sense that an entire philosophical tendency from Antonio Rosmini to Capograssi (to cite only the Italians) was oriented.

Second, for me the metaphysics of being is not identified at all with deductive philosophizing; rather, it is an inquiry that pro-ceeds from the analysis of human experience in all the richness of its manifestations in order to arrive at the understanding of its roots. Such an inquiry, then, goes from the phenomenological analysis to the ontological interpretation.

From this philosophical perspective the specific theme of this book is enlightened in its essential terms, which are here syn-thesized. Without the reference to being (mine and the Other's), to the being appearing in the intraworldly and ultraworldly on-tological relationship, there is no way out of the circuit of vio-lence, and as a result it inevitably remains the essential point for understanding man's identity. Rather than appearing as that which is judicable according to the measure of our being, violence ap-pears as that which ultimately measures our human stature: the more or less "strong will" of Nietzsche, the more or less "free desire" of libertine thought (from Sade to Deleuze), the major and minor "power" of the Prince, whether Machiavellian or Hob-besian, Leninist or Gramscian, and so on. Thus, while the meta-physics of subjectivity obliterates the specific physiognomy of violence to the point of disguising it under the mask of freedom and liberation, the metaphysics of being permits us to understand its peculiar consistency and destructiveness.

It would, however, be naïve to think that violence, brought to light in the face of being, vanishes as does a nightmare. It is and remains a real possibility, inborn in the *finite* and *defective* human condition. It serves no purpose to deny it or to deny its connec-tion with the death impulse whose presence has also been pointed out since Freud in psychoanalytic language. What concerns us is to see that violence be revealed by reflection not as the *only*, but simply as *one* human possibility: that which realizes itself in an immediate and passional reaction to varied encounters without re-ciprocal understanding between empirical events and sensibilities;

and that which remains unresponsive to the call for relationship coming from the ontological structures—the possibility that is always a latent snare but not an unavoidable fatality. In this reflective frame of mind it is possible to find a sure way of resisting its temptation and of preventing its rise.

As I have shown in the preceding chapters, there undoubtedly lies on this path the renunciation of violence in favor of force, which is opposed to the violence in its structure, as measure opposes excessiveness. The acquisition of the juridical sense understood in its full existential meaning lies even more markedly on the same path. The law, in fact, admits force, but, not confining itself to measured *activity-contra*, subordinates and directs it to a higher measure, that of *activity-pro:* the development of the subjects in the well-balanced and regular coordination of their actions. Measure here expresses its own highest value as a custodian and caretaker of a peaceful and solidaristic existence.

However, neither the sense of force nor that of the law is yet sufficient to uproot violence from its foundation. In this world of rule (albeit the rule of being and of justice) unruliness can still continue to rebel, contesting against any reason the foundation of the rule itself, and therefore of the balance and the duration, as Nietzsche did.[1] In its delirium, it may invent like Deleuze a fanciful cha-osmos, the chaotic order; or, in a more activistic way, it may continue to pursue the revolutionary myth of a purifying and regenerating destruction. It may, in short, persist in proposing the dream of a future being, all new and free from the measuring ontological relation, and so justify violence.

For the radical reversal of violence, then, it is necessary to draw from the experience of being something more than the sense of force and law. Max Weber wrote very penetratingly on this subject: "The universal experience that violence always generates violence, that violence against injustice leads in the end not to the victory of a higher justice but to a greater force and astuteness . . . promotes the ever radical request of the ethics of brother-

1. Cf. *Der Wille zur Macht* (Kroener edition, 1964), pp. 376, 432, where the concepts of duration and balance are rejected as not proved.

hood, of never meeting evil with violence."[2] These are words that repeat in our century, through the mouth of a thinker of socialist persuasion, the eternal words of the Gospel. Excessiveness is not radically overcome by measure, but by what is beyond measure itself: charity.

It would, however, be erroneous to consider this as a purely moral call or, still worse, as one sentimentally moralistic. Charity has its own roots in the most intimate regions of being, where not only the structural rationality manifests itself but so also does the vital need (inseparable from it) that such a relation be willed and, therefore, confirmed and promoted in actuality in the varied experience of life. One cannot preserve being without loving it in the existents in which it reveals itself. Therefore, reflection on being discovers in it, besides the source and the reason for the conceptual, theoretical negation of violence, the source and the reason for the personal commitment to a life, which transcends it. The genuinely radical answer to the excessiveness of violence, which seizes everything for the benefit of the egocentric subject, is that of the superabundance of charity. With it the *I* opens up totally to the Other under the sign of a gift and of forgiveness, which presuppose measure but go beyond it in a personal encounter all to be discovered and renewed in every moment. The plenitude of *agape* is thus disclosed: the joy of the living-together beyond any asperity and contradiction of finite existence.

2. Weber, *Economia e società* (Milan, 1961), 1 : 580.

Selected references

Here are listed the original-language titles, their English translations, and, where appropriate, the Italian editions of works frequently cited in the text.

Alain [Chartier, Émile]. 1952. *Politique* [Politics]. Paris.
Arendt, Hannah. 1970. *On Violence* [*Sulla violenza;* Milan, 1971]. New York.
Armellini, S. 1976. *Saggi sulla premialità del diritto nell'età moderna* [Essays on the rewarding nature of law in the modern age]. Rome.
Augustine, Saint. *De civitate Dei* [City of God] (*Opera omnia* vol. 7, in Migne *Patrologia latina*, Paris, 1841–77).
Bakunin, Mikhail. 1968. *Libertà e rivoluzione* [Liberty and revolution]. Naples.
Benjamin, Walter. 1962. *Angelus Novus.* Turin.
Bobbio, N. 1970. *Studi per una teoria generale del diritto* [Studies for a general theory of law]. Turin.
———. 1977. *Dalla struttura alla funzione* [From structure to function]. Milan.

Breton, André. 1935. *La position politique du surréalisme* [The political position of surrealism]. Paris.

Brun, Jean. 1973. *La nudité humaine* [Human nakedness]. Paris.

_____. 1976. *Les vagabonds de l'Occident* [The vagabonds of the West]. Paris.

Camus, Albert. 1951. *L'homme révolté* [The rebel]. Paris.

Capograssi, G. 1921. *Riflessioni sull'autorità e la sua crisi* [Reflections on authority and its crisis] (Milan, 1977).

Cesa, C. 1976. *Hegel filosofo politico* [Hegel, political philosopher]. Naples.

Cotta, Sergio. 1942. *Prospettive di filosofia del diritto* [Perspectives of philosophy of the law]. 2d ed. Turin.

_____. 1953. "Per un concetto giuridico di rivoluzione" [For a juridical concept of revolution] in *Scritti in onore di Luigi Sturzo* [Essays in honor of Luigi Sturzo]. Rome.

_____. 1970. "Rivoluzione e rivolta" [Revolution and revolt]. *Proteus* 1: 3–10.

_____. 1971. *La sfida tecnologica* [The technological challenge]. 4th ed. Bologna.

_____. 1972. *Itinerari esistenziali del diritto* [Existential itineraries of the law]. Naples.

_____. 1975. La sexualité en tant que dernier mythe politique. *Res Publica* 17 (1975): 357–66.

_____. 1975. *L'uomo tolemaico* [The Ptolemaic man]. Milan.

_____. 1977. "L'attuale ambiguità dei diritti fondamentali." *Rivista di diritto civile* 22: 225–42.

Del Grande, Carlo. 1947. *Hybris*. Naples.

Del Noce, A. 1965. *Riforma cattolica e filosofia moderna, I: Cartesio* [Catholic reformation and modern philosophy. I: Descartes]. Bologna.

Ellul, Jacques. 1969. *Autopsie de la révolution* [Autopsy of revolution; New York, 1971] (*Autopsia della rivoluzione;* Turin, 1974). Paris.

_____. 1975. *Sans feu ni lieu* [published in English under the title *The Meaning of the City*]. Paris.

Ferrero, Guglielmo. 1936. *Aventure. Bonaparte en Italie* [The gamble: Bonaparte in Italy]. Paris.

_____. 1940. *Reconstruction. Talleyrand à Vienne* [The reconstruction of Europe; Talleyrand and the Congress of Vienna]. Geneva-Paris.

———. 1944. *Pouvoir* [published in English under the title *The Principles of Power: The Great Political Crises of History*]. Paris.

Fiorelli, P. 1953–1954. *La tortura giudiziaria nel diritto comune* [Judiciary torture in common law]. Milan.

Fisichella, D. 1976. *Analisi del totalitarismo* [Analysis of totalitarianism]. Messina-Florence.

Flick, G. M. 1972. *La tutela della personalità nel delitto di plagio* [The protection of personality in the crime of plagiarism]. Milan.

Freud, Sigmund. 1929. *Das Unbehagen in der Kultur [Civilization and its discontents; London, 1930] (Il disagio della civiltà e altri saggi;* Turin, 1971). Vienna.

Frosini, V. 1962. *La struttura del diritto* [The structure of the law]. Milan.

Habermas, J. 1962. *Strukturwandel der Öffentlichkeit* [Structural change of public opinion] (*Storia e critica dell' opinione pubblica;* Bari, 1971). Neuwied.

Hegel, G. W. F. 1807. *Phänomenologie des Geistes* [Phenomenology of mind] (*Fenomenologia dello spirito;* Florence: 1970).

———. 1821. *Grundlinien der Philosophie des Rechts* [Philosophy of right] (*Filosofia del diritto;* Bari, 1971).

Heidegger, Martin. 1954. *Vorträge und Aufsätze* [Lectures and essays]. Pfullingen.

Huizinga, Johan. 1919. *Herfstij der Middeleeuwen* [Waning of the Middle Ages] (*L'autunno del Medio Evo;* Florence, 1966). Haarlem.

Kelsen, Hans. 1960. *Reine Rechtslehre* [Pure doctrine of law; Berkeley, 1967] (*La dottrina pura del diritto;* Turin, 1966). 2d ed. Vienna.

Kierkegaard, Søren. 1909–1948. *Dagboger* [Journals] (*Diario;* Brescia, 1963). Copenhagen.

Lenin, Vladimr Ilyich. 1917. *Gosudarstvo i revolyutsiya* [State and revolution; London, 1933] (*Stato e rivoluzione;* Rome, 1963). Leningrad.

———. 1949. *Opere scelte* [Selected works]. Moscow.

Lombardi Vallauri, L. 1976. *Abortismo libertario e sadismo* [Libertarian abortionism and sadism]. Milan.

Marx, Karl. 1950. *Opere filosofiche giovanili* [Early philosophical works]. Ed. L. Firpo. Rome.

_____. 1950. *Scritti politici giovanili* [Early political writings]. Turin.

Mathieu, V. 1972. *La speranza nella rivoluzione* [The hope of revolution]. Milan.

Merleau-Ponty, Maurice. 1947. *Humanisme et terreur* [Humanism and terror] (1974 edition cited here). Paris.

Montanari, B. 1976. *Obiezione di coscienza* [Conscientious objection]. Milan.

Montesquieu, Charles Louis de Secondat. 1748. *Esprit des lois* [The spirit of laws].

Muller, Jean-Marie. 1967. *Le défi de la nonviolence* [The challenge of nonviolence] (*Il significata della nonviolenza*). Paris.

Nietzsche, Friedrich. 1872. *Die Geburt der Tragödie* [The birth of tragedy].

_____. 1883–1891. *Also Sprach Zarathustra* [Thus spake Zarathustra] (*Così parlò Zarathustra;* Milan, 1976).

_____. 1886. *Jenseits von Gut und Böse* [Beyond good and evil] (*Al di là del bene e del male;* Milan, 1968).

_____. 1901. *Der Wille zur Macht* [Will to power].

Ortega y Gasset, José. 1967. *Obras completas* [Compete works]. Madrid.

Pascal, Blaise. 1670. *Pensées* [published in English under the title *Thoughts: an Apology for Christianity*] (Hachette; Paris: 1897).

Pasqualucci, P. 1976. *Rousseau e Kant* [Rousseau and Kant]. Milan.

Pekelis, A. 1930. *Il diritto come volontà costante* [Law as a constant will]. Padua.

Piovani, P. 1972. *Principi di una filosofia morale* [Principles of a moral philosophy]. Naples.

Polin, R. 1977. *La liberté de notre temps* [The liberty of our times]. Paris.

Romano, B. 1976. *La liberazione politica* [Political liberation]. Ancona.

Rousseau, Jean Jacques. 1959. *Œuvres complètes* [Complete works]. Pléiade edition. Paris.

Sartre, Jean Paul. 1943. *L'être et le néant* [Being and nothingness]. Paris.

_____. 1951. *Le Diable et le bon Dieu* [The devil and the good Lord]. Paris.

_____. 1960. *Critique de la raison dialectique* [Critique of dialectical reason]. Paris.

Scheler, Max. 1923. *Wesen und Formen der Sympathie* [The nature of sympathy]. (Bern edition of 1973 cited here.) Bonn.

Simmel, Georg. 1921. *Der Konflikt der modernen Kultur* [The conflict in modern culture] (*Il conflitto dell cultura moderna;* Rome, 1976).

Solovyov, Vladimir. 1900. *Tri razgovora* [published in English under the title *Three Dialogues on War, Progress, and the End of History*] (*Tre dialoghi sulla guerra, il progresso e la fine della storia universale;* Turin, 1975).

Sorel, Georges. 1908. *Réflexions sur la violence* [Reflections on violence]. 5th ed. Paris, 1921.

Stoppino, M. 1973. "Gli usi politici della violenza" [The political use of violence]. *Il Politico* 38:449–53.

Treitschke, Heinrich von. 1897. *Politik* [Politics]. Leipzig.

Trotsky, Leon. 1923. *Literature i revolyuciya* [Literature and revolution] (*Letteratura e rivoluzione;* Turin, 1973). Moscow.

———. 1958. *Letteratura, arte, libertà* [Literature, art, freedom]. Milan.

Vladimov, Georgiy. 1975. *Vernyi Ruslan* [The faithful Ruslan] (*Il fedele Ruslan*).

Weber, Max. 1956. *Wirtschaft und Gesellschaft* [*Economy and society;* New York, 1968] (*Economia e società;* Milan, 1961). Tübingen.

Weil, Simone. 1948. *La pesanteur et la grâce* [Gravity and grace]. Paris.

———. 1953. *La source grecque* [published in English under the title *Intimations of Christianity among the Ancient Greeks*] (*La Grecia e le intuizioni precristiane:* Turin, 1967). Paris.

Index

147